RESTORATION

Also by Faith Winters

Trauma Healing Series - Book 2

RESTORATION

Living as Designed, in Joy and Peace

Faith Winters

www.FaithfulHabits.com

Trauma Healing Series - Book 2

RESTORATION: Living as Designed, in Joy and Peace

Author: Faith Winters

First Printing: August 2021

Paperback ISBN: 978-1-7367367-8-4

Library of Congress Control Number

Faithful Habits Press

www.faithfulhabits.com

Editor: Rochelle Dean

Cover Art by Evelyn Drambarean

Contact the author at: Author@faithfulhabits.com

To order bulk copies for groups contact: Info@faithfulhabits.com

About the author

 **Faith Winters** is a mental health professional with nearly two decades of experience. She is an expert who has taught thousands of people how to live calmer, more fulfilling lives. She is an author of books focused on helping people to heal and grow. Faith has mentored and trained many other mental health professionals.

Why I wrote this Trauma Healing Book Series

I grew up in an abusive home. The childhood wounds to our hearts and self-worth rarely heal on their own. They need some intentional help to heal. As a child, I learned ways to cope with the wounds. While those coping mechanisms allowed me to survive as a child, those same learned habits crippled my life as an adult and made each day harder than it needed to be. The wounds of the past were not healed, just buried. To heal I needed to learn the fundamental principles of how to live a healthy life that removes barriers to growth. Through a healing process, I learned how to value myself, how to have boundaries with others and how to find the freedom of wise decision-making. Now I live a calm, happy life with a calling to help others to escape the pains of the past.

God has comforted me, and I want to help others be comforted as they heal and grow. I want there to be less suffering in the world. My journey has uniquely qualified me to help others move toward a healthier life.

- **Experience in living for decades with struggles** – I grew up in traumatic circumstances and spent decades as an adult dealing with anxiety, panic attacks, and PTSD (Post Traumatic Stress Disorder). In the midst of those painful years, I learned valuable lessons in surviving struggles and the need for healing.
- **Healing process** – I went through psychoeducational classes, extensive reading, and professional mental health therapy. As my anxiety ended, and the panic attacks ceased, and the PTSD was finally gone, I wanted to help others to escape the traumas of the past and to heal and grow.
- **Education** – I then decided to attend university to get a master's degree in counseling so I would have the professional therapeutic skills to help others heal from trauma in effective ways.
- **Experience in teaching these key skills to others** – For nearly two decades I have worked as a professional counselor and have taught thousands of people how to deal with struggles, heal from trauma and live calmer, healthier, happier lives even in the midst of struggles.

As you learn more about your rights as a human, your mind may experience a shift from being a victim of trauma toward the possibility of a happy and healthy life. All of the principles in this book will help to build strength within you as you grow and heal. It will take some effort on your part to live out your rights and responsibilities, but the principles to move forward are here in your hands. If you apply these principles, it may literally change the course of your life and have a positive effect on people around you.

In these pages, I share the richness of our original design and how to remove the crippling effects of past traumas so you can heal. I provide tried-and-true methods for how you can make changes to let yourself heal from the wounds of your past and the fundamental principles of our original design of how we can heal and grow. If you address the emotional, physical, and intellectual principles presented in this book, you can have a healthier life. By learning and enacting the principles of a healthy lifestyle, you can live your very best life, unhindered by the debilitating effects of past traumas. If you learn and apply these principles, it can literally change the course of your life and have a positive effect on people around you. you will discover a revolution inside, a return to something even more powerful than happiness. That is the presence of peace.

Trauma Healing Series Outline

www.TraumaHealingSeries.com

This **Trauma Healing Series** explores the differences between a healthy, functional life and a wounded life impacted by the lingering effects of bullying, abuse, trauma, neglect, domestic violence, substance use, and chaos. The series is designed to help lower the barriers that hinder growth and healing so you can move forward toward the freedom of thriving.

> *Trauma is any disturbing experience* that results in significant fear, helplessness, dissociation, confusion, or other disruptive feelings intense enough to have a long-lasting negative effect on a person's attitudes, behavior, and other aspects of functioning. Traumatic events may challenge a person's view of the world as a reasonable, safe, and predictable place.

Many individuals experience trauma during their lifetimes. Although some people exposed to trauma demonstrate few lingering symptoms, other people— especially those who have experienced repeated, chronic, or multiple traumas—are more likely to have many struggles and after-effects, including emotional distress, substance abuse, and physical and mental health problems.

Many individuals who seek help and recovery have histories of trauma. But they often do not recognize the impact their trauma has had on their lives. Either they do not draw connections between their past trauma and their current struggles, or they may try to avoid thinking about hard times altogether. Time alone does not heal most trauma; healthy processing is a part of the healing dynamic.

> **Processing the past** is the act of making sense of an experience and putting it to rest, which includes achieving the resolution needed to move on from a traumatic experience. If some aspect of trauma is not processed, it may continue to cause problems in the present until it can be put to rest.

Books in the Trauma Healing Series

Trauma Healing Series - Book 1

FUNDAMENTALS

Escape the Lingering Effects of Bullying, Abuse or Trauma

By learning your fundamental human rights, developing inner awareness of your strengths, and understanding the contrast to past chaos you will step into a life with security, significance, and happiness. Explore how to have more peace within yourself, better relationships with others, and more freedom and contentment, no matter what is going on around you.

Trauma Healing Series - Book 2

RESTORATION

Living as Designed, in Joy and Peace

You are designed to have peace and joy and be able to heal from the wounds of life. Look deeply into your uniqueness. Put to rest the old wounds that hinder your healing and trap you into painful patterns of responding to life. By exploring and adopting healthy patterns instead, you will live your best life after trauma. You will have restoration.

Trauma Healing Series - Book 3

CONNECTIONS

Master the Art of Relationship

When you do what it takes to develop wholesome social habits and essential boundary skills, you can have good relationships at home, at work, and with friends, family, and that special someone, no matter what your past relationships were like. By learning key skills for a healthy lifestyle and safe, healthy relationships, you will unlock the power of community to discover your connected place in the world.

Trauma Healing Series - Book 4

ABUNDANCE

Create Confidence, Contentment and Happiness

You can have the freedom of contentment, recognizing and enjoying the abundance of life around you. Contentment is not the fulfillment of what you want but the realization of what you already have. By using the principles of abundance in this book, you will derive riches that go far beyond the temporary rewards of success and create lasting happiness in any situation.

Table of Contents

WHAT THIS BOOK IS ABOUT

We are designed to heal. When you get a cut on your finger, it will start a healing process right away to be restored to its original design. If nothing hinders it, healing will soon take place. If it has a sliver, dirt, or germs in it, your body still works towards healing, but there is matter in the way that hinders complete healing. The wound needs cleaning out to have the full, healthy healing process work properly. It is similar with mental and emotional healing from a troubled past. The lingering effects of bullying, abuse, trauma, trouble, or chaos can negatively affect the healing process. It affects today's relationships, today's ability to make good decisions, and today's ability to have joy. To heal properly, the trauma wounds need cleaning.

Many people have experienced trauma and problems in their life that create pain, chaos, and lingering emotional wounds. The negative patterns of behavior that follow these wounds can last for decades. The wounds are rarely healed by time alone. Understanding our original design and changing to a healthy pattern of behavior, then removing the barriers that hinder our progress, will give those wounds a good chance to heal.

This book explores our basic design as a person of worth and the way past trauma hinders our individual healing. We are designed to have the joy of a rich emotional life and a creative mind. We are designed to heal from the wounds of life. However, to heal, our trauma wounds need to be cleaned out. We will look deeply into the way old wounds can erode your self-worth and trap you into painful patterns of responding to life that hinder your healing. Then we will explore your uniqueness, healthy patterns of living, and how to move from wounded toward health.

Restoration was written to help people to build insight into their own inner value and to help them to learn healthy ways of functioning. The second book in the Trauma Healing Series, *Restoration* will give an in-depth look at the primary principles on which a healthy life is based, the way we are designed to function, and how to heal. The other three books in the series—*Fundamentals*, *Connections*, and *Abundance* —explore the foundational principles of healing and then go deeply into the skill-building process in relationships and personal freedom in healing old wounds and moving into a pattern of healthy living.

About the Author

As a child, I grew up in an abusive home, and I learned ways to cope with the trauma. While those coping skills were functional ways that allowed me to survive as a child, those same learned habits crippled my life as an adult and made each day harder than it needed to be. The childhood wounds to our heart and self-worth often will not heal on their own; they need some intentional help to heal. We need to learn how to live the type of healthy life that removes barriers to healing. Through a healing process, I learned how to value myself, how to have boundaries with others, and how to find the freedom of wise decision-making. Now I live a calm, happy life with a career and calling to help others to escape from the pains of the past.

The solution to a traumatic history is not "just forget the past." The solution is putting the past to rest so old coping patterns do not hinder your present. This means learning how to build and strengthen within yourself the resilience to face life's troubles with healthy and unshakable confidence.

Praise be to the God and Father of our Lord Jesus Christ, the Father of compassion and the God of all comfort, who comforts us in all our troubles, so that we can comfort those in any trouble with the comfort we ourselves receive from God.

2 Corinthians 1:3-4

YOUR RIGHTS AS A HUMAN BEING

In the first book of this trauma healing series, *FUNDAMENTALS*, we explored in depth our basic rights as humans. In this second book , *RESTORATION*, we are building on those foundational principles.

Individual rights include how we interact with ourselves, the boundaries we set up, and understanding what is our own and what is not ours. Individual rights include the basic ways we can expect to be treated and the basic ways we treat others, with dignity and respect.

- You have the right to be you and love and be loved.
- You have the right to make mistakes, to be human – not perfect.
- You have the right to say NO.
- You have the right to choose your own values and beliefs.
- You have the right to your own feelings and opinions and to express them.
- You have the right to change your mind and your life.

Relational rights are the rights that we have as we relate to other people: family, friends, children, a significant other, parents, bosses, neighbors, and all the different people that we interact with in life. The healthy ways to interact with people.

- You have the right to be safe, to be treated with dignity and respect.
- You have the right to treat yourself as well as you treat others.
- You have the right to choose your own friends.
- You have the right to choose when and how your body is touched.
- You have the right not to be responsible for other's choices, feelings, and behavior.
- You have the right to feel angry and protest if you are treated abusively.

Freedom rights are the freedoms that we have individually and collectively to make our own choices of what we want to do and how we want to move forward in our life. These are the responsibilities and choices we have as adults.

- You have the right to your own privacy, personal space, and time.
- You have the right to make your own decisions about your life.
- You have the right to ask questions about anything that affects your life.
- You have the right to ask for what you want.
- You have the right to earn and control your own resources.
- You have the right to not be liked by everyone.

Restoration
The act of bringing back to a former position or condition, restoring to an unimpaired or improved condition, replacement or giving back of something that was lost.

PART ONE

Restoration Of Design In My Heart

We talk of the heart when we actually mean our emotions. The first part of *Restoration* is about the wide ration of emotions we are designed to feel as human beings. Our emotions help us to understand each other and to understand God in deeper and richer ways. When we have been affected by trauma, it can wound our ability to fully access our emotions. But restoration and healing are available for you. We are designed to heal.

CHAPTER 1

The Design – Vibrant Emotional Life

A life without emotions would seem sterile, or black and white. Our lives were designed to be healthy, rich, and vibrant. We are created in the image of God. God has emotions. He created us to feel emotions. Our full range of emotions is normal and natural.

Then God said, "Let us make mankind in our image, in our likeness...
Genesis 1:26

Some of God's emotions:

- **Compassion** – When Jesus landed and saw a large crowd, he had compassion on them and healed their sick.

  Matthew 14:14

- **Sadness** – Jesus wept.

  John 11:35

- **Love** – For God so loved the world that he gave his one and only Son, that whoever believes in him shall not perish but have eternal life.

    John 3:16

- **Delight** – For the Lord takes delight in his people...

    Psalm 149:4

- **Hate** – There are six things the Lord hates, seven that are detestable to him:

    Proverbs 6:16

- **Anger** – Then the Lord's anger burned against Moses.

    Exodus 4:14

- **Joy** – May the glory of the Lord endure forever; may the Lord rejoice in his works.

    Psalm 104:31

- **Pleasure** – The Lord was pleased that Solomon had asked for this.

    1 Kings 3:10

Emotions are a wonderful part of the human experience. But sometimes our emotions can feel overwhelming, especially to someone who has experienced trauma. Our coping response may have been to try to avoid feeling emotions or to use something to try to blunt our emotions. The healing we are designed to experience is not to avoid feeling emotions. Healing is about learning how to handle emotions in a healthy way.

How a child learns about gravity

A way to understand how we can learn to handle emotions in a healthy way is to think about how a baby learns to walk. At first, it is a struggle for the baby to try to stand. The child falls and gravity pulls them down and they struggle to stand up again. A nurturing mother encourages her little son to try again. Gravity pulls him down again and he bumps his nose and cries. Mom continues encouraging him to struggle, to try again, and gravity keeps pulling him down. His mother keeps encouraging because mom knows that through that very struggle, his legs will strengthen and his ability to balance will increase. Soon he will have the freedom of walking and running. He will even learn how to play with gravity as he bounces balls and goes down slides. Gravity has not changed; only his ability to handle gravity has changed.

It is like that with emotions that seem overwhelming at first and we do not want to deal with them. Some of the emotions are painful. Some emotions may even seem scary. The way to escape the difficulty of the painful or overwhelming emotions is not to push them away or ignore them. If we do, the feelings are still there waiting for us. It takes a lot of effort to avoid them. In some ways, it is like holding an air-filled beach ball underwater. Although it takes a bit of effort we can do it, at least until we get tired or distracted. Then, at the worst possible moment, our hold on it slips and it pops up and hits us in the face. Emotions can be like that. We can suppress what we feel for a time, until we get tired, stressed, or distracted. Then, in the worst possible moment, emotions overwhelm our control and burst out.

The way to escape the difficulties of emotions is to struggle through them and learn how to embrace your emotions and integrate them into your life. Then you will have the freedom of a rich emotional life and you will even learn to play with your emotions. For instance, when you go to the movies, you are letting the movie take you on an emotional ride. You are then playing with your emotions.

Love is a core emotion that drives so much of our behavior that it is the focus of this chapter. People will do things for love they will not likely do for any other emotion. We all yearn to love and be loved.

Love is a primary emotion. We are designed to love and be loved. Love is also one of the primary emotions to suffer the traumatic wound of perceived betrayal. Betrayal comes in many forms. The first one we may think of is the unfaithfulness of a significant other. When you thought you had a faithful, committed relationship, you found they were not committed to you and they were with someone else; this betrayal can make it hard to trust someone enough to love again,

Why is it hard to love if you have been betrayed?

There are also other betrayals that wound our ability to love. When a child has been abused, especially if the abuser was a trusted caregiver, that is a deep betrayal that shakes a child's view of the world and understanding of how love works in the world. When an abuser tells the child 'I love you' and sexually abuses the child, that is confusing to a child and makes all messages about 'love' feel dangerous and untrustworthy.

Betrayal of love can even hurt the victim's relationship with God. *Why didn't God protect me?* Or, if the child was abused by the one in the role of father, and one of the ways God is referred to is our Heavenly Father, the child can think those two individuals are alike and since her daddy was not trustworthy her heavenly Father might not be trustworthy either.

And yet we all yearn for love, to be deeply connected. To love and be loved is one of our deepest desires. What exactly is 'love' and what does that word mean? In English, we use one word for love. We use it to say, "I love my spouse," "I love my child," "I love the color green," and "I love to eat pizza." Despite using one word, those are different kinds of love. And there is another kind of love that is not even an emotion. Altruistic love is doing what is in the best interest of others. Being deeply connected with others is a part of our original design.

Defining Love – in English: a great interest and pleasure in something.

Here are four concepts from the Greek language that describe types of love:

- *Eros* – romantic, passionate love, from which we get our English word "erotic." Attraction based on sexual desire, affection, and tenderness felt by lovers.
- *Storge* – familial love, referring to natural or instinctual affection, such as the love of a parent toward offspring and children toward parents and siblings.
- *Philia* – the affectionate bond of friends, from which we get the name of the city "Philadelphia," the "city of brotherly love." It is about commitment, the love that binds one to

5

another in enduring friendship, and strong affection for another.

- *Agape* – unconditional, self-sacrificing love that seeks the welfare of the other. Unselfish loyal and benevolent concern for the good of another, to do what is in the long-term best interest of another. Not just a feeling, but a choice of will.

To be loved by another is a great pleasure. There is a wonderful safety, a sense of belonging, and of finding a 'home' in love. Home is not so much a place as it is the people who love and accept you for who you are and who encourage and support you.

Being betrayed can cause someone to question if they are even deserving of love. They can worry that something is so wrong with them that no one could ever love them. That is a lie of the old trauma wound. Everyone deserves to love and be loved. 'Unlovable' is a false message of the trauma of the past, not a truth of the present.

In summary

Emotions are a gift we have been given. Emotions are a part of our original design of the image of God in us. The primary emotion is love. Everyone has the right to love and be loved.

CHAPTER 2

Grief and loss

Emotions are designed to bring a depth of feeling even when joy is contrasted with grief. We can endure the sad or painful times, knowing joy will come again. Not only were we given emotions, but we are also designed to heal through emotions.

Common Losses

Life is hard, and then we die. While we still live, there are many types of losses we experience throughout our lives. Some common losses are the death of a loved one, loss of a job, loss of health, loss of safety, loss of a home, loss of our view of the world as a safe place, loss of a beloved pet, loss of the defined role as nurturing parent as children grow up and move out, loss of my view of myself as young and vibrant as I grow older, grayer, and ache more, and many other losses, big and small.

Changes affect people in different ways. In her 1969 book *On Death and Dying*, Elizabeth Kubler-Ross suggested there are five stages of grief that people go through denial, anger, bargaining, depression, and acceptance. However, grief is not a linear process and people can circle in and out of any of the stages at different times in their lives.

Let's look at aging for example. Some people see getting older as a "loss of youth," rather than a natural part of the life cycle. They deal with the loss of youth first by denying it is happening. You may see them get angry that they can no longer do some things as well that they could when they were young and physically stronger. They get angry and drive their bodies to retain the ability that youth have, thinking or bargaining that if I just do this exercise routine I will be able to keep the strength of my youth. It can seem to work for a while. But the years roll on. Then they may be sad about the changes their aging body is going through. Finally, they accept *this is who I am,* and they make a new life with the reality of how they look now and their physical capabilities. This is the stage when a calm acceptance of the joys of aging begin to filter in.

Another way people try to escape the pain of loss is by devaluing the relationship. If a cherished old vase breaks, they are in shock, then hardly believe it, then they may deny that it was ever cherished, saying it was old and a bother to care for anyway.

A Fox one day saw a beautiful bunch of ripe grapes hanging from a vine. The bunch hung from a high branch, and the Fox had to jump for it. But it was so high he could not reach then no matter how high he jumped. He finally stood looking at the grapes and said, "They are probably sour anyway." And he walked off. The moral is people often devalue what they cannot have. Aesop

A healthy way to deal with loss is to recognize the value of what was and allow yourself to grieve the loss of that value. Then accept the loss and move toward to the reality of what life is now.

Healthy ways to deal with loss include going through the stages of grief, but not getting stuck in any of them. They are *part* of a healthy grieving process, not a destination to stay at. Healing comes through pondering the loss and the feelings of loss and talking with safe people in a safe place. This allows us to process the grief, feel what we feel, and move forward toward integrating this event into our life. Then we can look at what life will be like moving into our future, past this loss.

The pain of a loss is a part of the grieving process. This pain will not always feel as sharp as it does at first. Allowing ourselves to grieve and feel the pain is normal and healthy. At first, it may feel like a raw and open wound. Later, as healing comes, it may be more like a healed scar. It will always be a part of our life, but without the sharp hurt that it contained at first.

Part of a healthy way to honor the value of something lost is to go on and live a full life, even incorporating some of the value of what you have learned by being able to enjoy what you had. When the loss is a loved one who died, one of the ways to honor their memory is to live a full life, even doing some of the things they cared about. For example: If your loved one valued travel, visit one of their favorite places. If they had a heart for animals, volunteer at a shelter. Remember them in a tangible, healthy way.

The tears of grief are normal, and a healthy part of washing clean the wound of grief. It is okay to let the tears flow. However, not all times and places are safe to weep. Perhaps we are at work months after the loss and people think we should be over it by now, yet we feel the sadness well up inside. When this happens, set yourself a safe time and place to let those tears flow. Perhaps after work when you can be alone or with someone it is safe to grieve with. There is no "normal" length of time for how long grieving takes. For some people, it may be longer than others. Just accept it for what it is and be kind to yourself. Make a time to meet with yourself and let the grief be felt.

Feeling sad is a normal part of life.

> *It is better to go to a house of mourning*
> *than to go to a house of feasting,*
> *for death is the destiny of everyone;*
> *the living should take this to heart.*
> *Proverbs 7:2*

In that house of mourning, we tend to ponder the fragility of life. How quickly it can end. It can make us think deeply about our own life. What are we doing that brings value to the earth? What are we doing that helps others? Are we the kind of person we want to be? When we take to heart that we will all die eventually, it can give us the motivation to tell those we love that we love them, that they have value and worth. It can remind us to settle disputes and not let arguments separate us. It can propel us to grow, learn, heal, and live an abundant life!

In summary

Integrating grief and loss into our lives allows the fullness of human experience to flow in us and therefore we grow and mature.

CHAPTER 3

Anxiety, fear, shame, and guilt

Anxiety, fear, shame, and guilt are neither good nor bad. They are neutral descriptions of emotional states. A functional level of any of these is capable of serving the purpose for which it was designed. It is designed to be good for a particular job or helping us operate in a specific way. A dysfunctional level of these emotions hinders rather than helps.

To err is human.

When we discover we have made a mistake we may feel anxiety, fear, shame, guilt, or a mix of all of those. Anxiety is a feeling of worry, nervousness, or unease, typically about a current event or something in the future with an uncertain outcome.

When a healthy person makes a mistake, it may produce a feeling of anxiety, disappointment, or maybe just a slight feeling of frustration or annoyance. A functional level of anxiety can be a source of strength, used as stimulation to be more aware, more diligent, and more alive.

But for other people, the feeling is more intense. A dysfunctional level of anxiety can disrupt daily life. This may include emotional distress, restlessness, fatigue, difficultly concentrating, irritability, tense muscles, and trouble sleeping. Some people even feel that to be wrong threatens their value in the world. They will fight diligently to prove they are not wrong, contrary to all evidence. Why is that?

If our worldview is that we have to be perfect to have value, then if we are found to be wrong, it means we have no value. We can end up feeling stupid like we are worthless. So, the natural response is to fight any hint of being wrong. However, this is an unhealthy coping mechanism.

In a healthy life, we understand that being wrong is generally a minor and repairable thing. In other words, an inconvenience that can be worked through and repaired. When repair is not possible, and it is a loss, there may be a cost to deal with, and forgiveness may need to be sought and costs paid. A healthy person can recognize this is not about the worth of a person who made the mistake, this is about the mistake itself. Those are two different things.

Being Wrong

What does it feel like to be wrong? It feels like being right. In an old cartoon, a roadrunner bird always runs, and a coyote chases him. In every episode, the bird runs off the edge of a high cliff and stands in midair for a moment. He is fine; he is a bird. But the coyote runs off the cliff right after him and stands there in midair for a moment too. Then the coyote looks down, realizes his danger, and falls. Being wrong is like that coyote at the moment he has run off the cliff, just before he looks down. He is already wrong, he is already going to deal with the consequences of being wrong, he just doesn't realize it yet. In that tiny moment, he feels right.

That is what it is like for us when we are wrong. We are already going to deal with the consequences of being wrong; we just do not know it yet. So being wrong feels like being right. If we would not try so hard to define every opinion we have as being the only way to be right, if we leave space for occasionally being wrong, life would be better for everyone and there would be a lot less conflict in the world.

Imagine you are looking at one side of a board that is standing on edge, someone else is looking at the other side. You see it as a brown board, and they say it is a blue board. Do you want to spend all your energy arguing what is the right color, or if you could talk a few moments to find out why they see it as blue and why you see it as brown? Perhaps even go look at the board from their perspective. You could see the blue color they saw. The argument is over and relationships would not be damaged.

Types of fear

Fear is a distressing feeling aroused by anticipation of danger or awareness of a threat, evil, pain, etc., whether the threat is real or imagined. Fear comes in more than one type. One type of fear is physical fear, the natural response of the physical body to extreme heights, for example. This type of fear is accompanied by an adrenaline rush and increased awareness. Another type of fear is mental fear. Something triggers it, and the mind flashes up thoughts of danger and harm and a threat to existence. Yet another type of fear happens when the mind constantly thinks about bad things that could happen and awareness is raised to such a level that they do not know which way to turn and are then immobile.

The common feature in all three of these types of fear is a heightened awareness and perhaps an adrenaline rush. These three types of fear could trigger all at once or separately from one another. Fear is a normal response to a perceived threat. Healthy fear is what keeps us from stepping in front of a speeding bus.

Unhealthy fear is when the perceived threat is in the mind at times when there is no threat, or perhaps our thoughts keep dwelling on a lot of negative what-ifs. This type of fear can be crippling. It hinders us from leaving our house. It makes it feel like a threat to life to walk across a street.

One way to cope and grow out of unhealthy fear includes writing down what you are afraid of, setting it aside, and coming back later to look at what you wrote down. This allows you to examine the truth of your perceptions of that fear. Ask yourself, "Is this true?" "Is this likely?" Plan out strategies for how to handle situations that trigger feelings of fear. Working through these with a mental health counselor can be very beneficial. Building key skills to being calm can help greatly as you work through fears.

For more on learning Seven key skills to being calm in the midst of troubling times go to:

www.FaithfulHabits.com/KeepingCalm

You will find a FREE guide to being calmer in 10 minutes.

Shame

Shame is a painful feeling of humiliation or distress caused by knowing a choice or behavior was wrong. Functional shame is a healthy response to doing something wrong or foolish. Healthy repair is to own it, confess, and ask what you can do to make it right, ask for forgiveness. Dysfunctional shame is the feeling that I am wrong, not that I *did something* wrong, but that I am a damaged human, and I am wrong.

Truth releases us from the trap of shame. Many people try to deal with shame by hiding the source of the shame, yet that keeps them trapped in a place when they are tormented by the shame. Confession can release us from the trap of shame. Yes, exposing the truth is likely to be awkward, messy, and uncomfortable. But so is staying stuck in shame. Living in truth can release us from the painful life affected by shame. Owning our faults and our mistakes can make them less painful to live with and leave space for happiness to fill our lives.

Guilt

Guilt is a feeling of unease due to having done something wrong or failed in an obligation that violates a standard of conduct, especially violating the law and involving a penalty, like when we sin against God and others. We are only guilty of the choices we make ourselves. We do not have to stay stuck in our guilt.

> *If we confess our sins,*
> *he is faithful and just*
> *and will forgive us our sins*
> *and purify us*
> *from all unrighteousness.*
> *1 John 1:9*

True guilt is the guilt I feel for a wrong I have done. I feel the guilt and it can drive me to do something about it, like confess it to God. Then I am released from the guilt. I may still have a repair to do to make it right with people, but God and I have worked it out. Confession is me agreeing with God that the behavior was wrong. I repent, turning away from guilty choices and asking his forgiveness.

If you put your finger on a hot stove, your nerve endings will send signals of pain to your brain, letting you know that you are hurting yourself and you need to remove your finger from the damaging source of that hurt. Guilt is like spiritual nerve endings. When we do something wrong, our conscience sends a message of pain/guilt to our brain telling us that we are damaging ourselves and others. You need to remove yourself from causing the damage and seek to repair.

Some people feel guilty all the time. They feel guilty for anything wrong in the world. That false guilt can be part of the worldview that an abuser leaves an abuse victim with. The abuser tells the victim they are responsible for the way the abuser is treating them. That shifting of blame is also a part of the abuse. The victim, especially if that victim is a child, may believe that lie, because the one in power is saying it. Even after the victim has escaped the abuse, and has grown to adulthood, they still may believe that they are responsible for the abuse that was done to them.

Unhealthy responsibility is when I had no choice in something, but I am made to feel I am responsible for another's choice: "It is your fault I did this." That is the message of a dysfunctional life, not the message of a healthy life. However, guilt is always an offer; we do not have to accept other people's offer of guilt. We are not guilty of what others do, only for choices we make ourselves.

In summary

Anxiety, fear, shame, and guilt are normal parts of a healthy life. But we do not have to have our life hindered by them. We can work through the emotions and what lies behind them and move forward to a life with joy, happiness, and peace.

CHAPTER 4

Joy, happiness, and peace

The pursuit of happiness

All of us want to feel happiness and joy. We have the right to pursue happiness. God designed our lives to have fun, happiness, pleasure, joy, and peace. What we do for work can bring us happiness, and what we do outside of work can bring us happiness. Our entertainment media is focused on fun, happiness, and enjoyment. We want to feel good feelings.

But the lingering effects of bullying, abuse, trauma, trouble, or chaos can leave us with a low-grade feeling of dread that wants to steal our happiness. We do not trust feeling happy. The very feeling itself may be unfamiliar, and the first time we feel it during our healing journey, we may be startled into thinking, "what is that feeling?" Or we may be used to only temporarily feeling good and never trust it to stay.

Part of the healing process can be learning to endure the feeling of happiness. We can learn to endure happiness for a moment, trust it for a moment. Like strengthening a muscle, exercise your ability to experience happiness to help it to heal and grow strong.

Let's explore the differences between a few types of pleasant feelings:

- **Happiness** is an enjoyable or satisfying feeling when life is pleasurable, feels good ,and promotes contentment. It covers a range of feelings from soft and pleasurable to intense and blissful. Happiness may show up after the fact.
- **Fun** is an amusement, enjoyment, or pleasure that is happening in the moment.
- **Pleasure** is an agreeable feeling that accompanies getting something good or much wanted. Pleasure is an internal feeling that may not show greatly externally.
- **Joy** is a deep welling of contentment and gladness that is not dependent upon our circumstances. Joy is there even in the midst of troubles. Joy is a stronger, more lasting feeling than happiness. Joy does not depend on circumstances.
- **Peace** is a state of being sound and complete, to have harmony and wholeness. It is the absence of strife or war. To make amends and put things right.

Sometimes people use substances to try to get a good feeling, only to find that the feeling is temporary and when it fades, they are less happy than they were before they used it. If they get addicted to a substance, the feeling-good times get shorter and less intense while the feeling-bad times coming down off the substance get longer and more intense. However, they continue to chase the short-term good feeling by using more and more substance. This is a downward spiral that does not end well. Substances are a cheat of happiness. Some people use relationships as a form of addiction in that same way.

When people use the response they get from other people as a way to get a good feeling a sense of worth they will find that is only a temporary feeling. It will soon fade, and they are seeking more input from that person, or input from more people to get the feeling again. They feel a deep hole they are trying to fill. This can become a type of relationship addiction.

The abyss

Many people feel like there is a deep abyss inside them that nothing can fill, a dark, hollow emptiness that saps their lives. We can try to fill it with substances, with relationships, with wealth, or with fame, but that deep, hollow feeling is still there. Anything we throw in there fills the abyss for a moment, but then it tears it wider. The truth is that abyss cannot be filled with anything. The solution to the abyss is not to fill it, but to heal it, so it will close and no longer be there. Often, we need a mental health professional to help us to process this chasm in a healing way. If we let God work in our wounded places, he will walk alongside us. If we follow his direction, he can heal that abyss and it will begin to get smaller and smaller. In place of it, we can have real peace and joy.

Real peace and joy are different from a mountaintop experience. Mountaintop experiences may feel euphoric, but we do not live in the rarified air of mountaintops. While we can visit there now and then, it is within the deep valleys where much of our growth takes place. That is where the rich soil and the fertilizer is that produce joy. Having more calm and peace in our life is a learned skill. There are many ways to learn key skills that will bring you more joy and peace.

Happiness is often a side effect of something else. We become focused on doing something, being with people, engaging in meaningful activities, and later, as we look back we can see that it was a very happy time. When we try to focus on just trying to be happy, happiness can elude us. When we try to live for the pleasure it can come to feel hollow and have no lasting happiness.

What makes you happy? Think back to a time when you felt happiness. What were you doing? Many people find that they were happy when accomplishing a hard task. Doing something that challenged them and was a struggle. And when they were done they had a calm sense of pleasure that felt rich and deep.

Other times we gain an enduring feeling of happiness being with people we care about and who care about us. The social connection itself brings us joy. It won't matter what we are doing, whether life is easy or hard, whether we have little or much. Happiness is loving and being loved.

In Summary

All of us want to feel happiness and joy, that is how God designed us. We want to feel good feelings. We can find those feelings through a sense of creativity and fulfillment in the work we do and the recreational actives we engage in. But the lingering effects of trauma can hinder our ability to enjoy those feelings, making it hard for us to trust feeling happy. Part of the healing process can be learning to endure happiness for a moment at a time. Like strengthening a muscle, exercise your ability to experience happiness to help it to heal and grow strong.

CHAPTER 5

Anticipation, disappointment, and gratefulness

The gift of anticipation

There is something to be said for living in the now and being fully alive to what is going on around you at this moment. But that is only part of a healthy life. There is also the anticipation of the future. Part of the happiness of a gift is the anticipation of what the future holds when we will open it. Part of the fun of the holiday season is the anticipation of the happiness the day will bring. The reason we wrap a gift is to add a little more joy of anticipation.

Disappointment is the feeling of sadness or displeasure of not getting what you expected or what you wanted or planned for. Disappointment comes when we are holding onto a specific desire of something we want and something else is given to us, and instead of enjoying what we received, we pine for what we thought we wanted. In that attitude of disappointment, we are hindering our own happiness.

When we hold our expectations lightly we still get to enjoy the anticipation, and if it doesn't turn out to be exactly what we had anticipated we are still free to look for the pleasure and benefit this new reality may bring.

Planning and holding plans flexibly.

There is an ancient military saying about plans. *"No plan lasts past the first engagement with the enemy [or reality]."* Having realistic expectations and plans, held flexibly, accounts for the normal changes and fluctuations of life, while still allowing us to be grateful and enjoy the benefits and pleasures around us now. It allows us to anticipate what the future may bring.

Unrealistic expectations that everything must go perfectly lead to disappointments that can interfere with our happiness. If 98 things went well and two things had problems, will we let those two problems steal our happiness from the other 98 things? Too often, the answer is yes.

Every Christmas, one family always said, "Who is going to ruin Christmas this year?" They started the holiday with the expectation that something was going to disappoint them, and this hindered their joy.

A healthy life expects problems will be mixed into the things that go well. We can strive for perfection, but be content with excellence, even be okay with just 'good enough.'

Blessed are the flexible, for they will not be broken.

Submitting to and accepting disappointment

Disappointment is a normal part of life. We anticipate what we hope will happen, and if it does not happen, we are disappointed. The healthy way to handle disappointment is to let yourself feel what you are feeling and observe these. Your behavior is still your choice. Your inner five-year-old may want to get mad and throw a tantrum, but this is where the mature adult you are gets to take a deep breath and calm down and remind your inner five-year-old that disappointments happen, and we need to accept them gracefully. It is a good time to remind yourself of the good things you still have and be grateful for what is good.

A woman who was very sick with a long-term illness would play a game every night: *What was good about today?* That simple question helped her to focus on finding and focusing on the good in each day.

We can have the joy of anticipation and hold it lightly, without counting on it. Then, if it does happen, we are delighted and if it does not happen, we may be disappointed, but not destroyed.

We are hard-pressed on every side, yet not crushed.
we are perplexed, but not in despair.
persecuted, but not forsaken.
struck down, but not destroyed—
2 Corinthians 4:8-9

When we anticipate the future, we can plan something we want to do then. The planning itself can bring us happiness. It can be fun to problem solve and see how things will work. We learn new stuff while working on the plans. Many times, our plans work out well. Include in your plans extra time and resources for the unexpected. Things often come up that need a little adjusting. If you have put extra time and resources into the plan, then the unexpected will not be as hard to deal with. It will not cause a crippling disappointment.

Plans are worthless, but planning is everything. There is a very great distinction because when you are planning for an emergency you must start with this one thing: the very definition of "emergency" is that it is unexpected, therefore it is not going to happen the way you are planning.

Dwight Eisenhower

The power of gratefulness

Being grateful for what you now have brings more happiness than being upset that you did not get what you wanted. A friend was asked one Sunday morning, "How are you doing?" Her answer was, "Fabulous!" I asked, "What is fabulous?" She replied, "I can get up by myself, feed myself, dress myself and ask for what I want."

In her work, she drove a school bus for those who could not do any of those things and it reminded her daily to be grateful for the blessings that she had. Small troubles or disappointments did not bother her because she was gratefully aware of the blessings she enjoyed each day. Joy or disappointment, your happiness or misery, is of your own choosing. Trouble is inevitable; misery is optional. Your choice.

In Summary

When we anticipate the good that will come to us, we feel pleasure, happiness. The anticipation itself brings happiness. Disappointments happen to everyone, but they do not have to make us miserable. When we choose to be more aware of the positive things in our lives and be grateful for what we have, we can live in the pleasure of gratitude.

CHAPTER 6

A rich emotional life

You have value. You are important. As we explored in the first chapter, you were created in the image of God, and God has emotions. He created you with these same emotions. The purpose of our emotions is for us to be able to have a rich, intimate relationship with God and each other, for us to connect with him in joy and worship, and for us to understand him more.

Healthy emotions

This is a day the Lord has made. We can choose to greet this day with rejoicing and gladness, or we can choose to greet it with dread and misery. When people say, "Well, it's Monday," the observation that it is Monday is neutral. But we put our own emotions onto it. I like to look at Monday as the start of a new week with no mistakes in it yet. Some people act like Monday is a horrible day, when they must start another hard week at work. You get to choose the joy of anticipation of something good or the misery of dreading something bad.

While it is good to choose to find joy where we can, it is also important to feel all of our emotions, even the sad ones. In Proverbs, it says better to go to a house of mourning than a house of feasting. In pondering why I think it is because when we are feasting and happy we may not thinking about our future and our growth. When we are in a house of mourning, we are reminded of the shortness of life, and it allows us to ponder: Am I the person I want to be? Am I doing the things that I want to do? It can be a time for us to evaluate our life and to take stock. We can ask ourselves: Am I cherishing the people who are still here whom I love? Have I told them that I love them? That they are important to me and what I appreciate about them? Am I telling them about the strengths I see in them, their growth, and the things in them I am proud of?

Ways to enrich emotional experiences.

Take the time to slow down and observe what you are feeling. Allowing yourself the freedom to feel enriches the pleasure in your life. Observing what we are feeling, and how that is expressed physically and mentally, increases our awareness of who we are and how we interact in the world. Observing where in your body you feel joy, where you feel anxiety, and where you feel delighted can enrich your experience of life. Even if what you are observing is sadness or grief, our emotions enrich our living experience. We feel more fully alive when we take those moments to observe ourselves. We may feel pensive or depressed at times, but we also feel happiness, curiosity, anticipation, disappointment, and a sense of satisfaction for a job well done. When we shut off from the risk of pain, we are also shutting ourselves off from many feelings of pleasure.

We can find delight by looking for and embracing small pleasures each day. Seeking beauty encourages joy and happiness. We have five senses which provide five different ways to enjoy life. Taking time to enjoy the color, texture, sight, smell and taste of food enriches our experience with food. If we only ate one single bland food all the time, it would not be a very nice experience. The same is true with emotions. If we only recognize one or two emotions or spend our days numb or in neutral, we miss out on life's abundant richness.

Another important skill in a rich emotional life is the ability to sit with discomfort. Life is not always comfortable, but we can still be at peace even within discomfort. The uncomfortable times will pass.

Weeping may stay for the night,
but rejoicing comes in the morning.
Psalm 30:5b

Part of a maturing emotional life is being able to feel okay with not knowing all the answers. Calmly looking at things without everything being exactly what we want or understand is an important skill. A fair amount of life is not black and white. Between black and white are the whole array of rich and beautiful colors.

When we make a mistake, we can feel complex emotions that may include embarrassment, shame, disappointment, and anxiety. The healthy way to handle a mistake is to own it, confess it, repair it, and try to move forward. That way our emotions can move through to a better place of feeling honest, resilient, faithful, and forgiven. If we try to hide the mistake or deny we made mistakes, we get trapped in our uncomfortable emotions. Truth is what releases us from the difficult emotional place.

The truth about our emotions is about being able to recognize what we are feeling and to be able to name the feelings and seek to understand where they are coming from. Many times, we need to observe our own emotions and pay attention to what we are feeling. Our emotions are giving us information, but that information is filtered through our past experiences. The emotion may or may not be a true reflection of what is actually going on right now.

Our emotions are often triggered by our senses:

Smell

Our sense of smell, the sensations we get from odors, can trigger emotions and maybe one of our strongest memory triggers. The same smell can trigger different emotions for different people. The fresh odor of a crushed mint leaf can trigger the pleasant emotions of being out of doors in a beautiful herb and flower garden for one person. For another, that same mint smell can trigger the uncomfortable memory of medicine and being ill in a hospital. The odor is neutral; how it affects us depends on our individual experiences.

Some of the things we smell are intense or rather pungent and strong; other odors are faint and wispy. Some are pleasant, some are unpleasant. With foods, the odor can draw us toward wanting to eat or turn us away in disgust. Our feelings arising from these smells please us or warn us of unpleasantness.

Touch

Feelings are also triggered by touch. Think about what you are touching right now. The slick feel of the screen of an electronic device, or the smoothness of paper. The sensation of the clothes you are wearing, the chair, or wall, or floor that you are touching. Be aware of all the different textures you are around right now. Some of them feel smooth and soft to the touch, others are coarse and heavy. What is your emotion when you touch these things? Is it pleasant? Is it uncomfortable? Is it neutral, just an observation?

Hearing

What do you hear right now? Do you hear the birds or the wind rustling in the leaves? What sounds are close by? Which ones are far away? What about sounds of vehicles or people going by or children's laughter? What sounds are pleasant to your ears? Which sounds are unpleasant? Which are neutral? Sounds can especially touch our emotions. Think of some of your favorite music. What emotions does that music trigger in you? When we are feeling sad, we may find solace in listening to melancholy music. When we are happy, we find joy in delightful tunes. We can even influence our emotions by the music we choose to listen to. When we are feeling sad, we may find comfort in listening to hope-filled music. Listening to depressing music about troubles may bring down our mood and influence us toward sadness. Music affects our emotions, and the words that are attached to the music can have an even greater impact on positive or negative emotions.

Seeing

Look around you right now. There is color everywhere. Which colors please your eyes? Which colors are neutral, which are intense, which are soft? What emotions do you feel when you look at a blue sky? What do you feel about the colors of grass and trees? What colors trigger pleasant emotions in you and which ones trigger unpleasant?

Taste

Think about your last meal. What were the different tastes involved? What was sweet? What was salty? What was spicy? What was mild? Foods are designed to give us pleasant sensations. What emotions did you feel while you were eating?

God designed us to experience joy. He gave us emotions so that we could feel happiness, pain, sorrow, accomplishment, and more, and all of these things enrich our experiences as human beings. God feels emotions as well. Our emotions remind us that we are created in his image and part of his image is a full range of rich emotions. That is part of the original design.

Free Resource - Guide to feelings vocabulary.

A helpful free resource showing images of feeling faces and a list of feeling words.

www.faithfulhabits.com

Includes over 500 words all from relating to emotions.

This guide will help equip you with how to explain your emotions to other people. When you have words to describe your emotions, it becomes easier to tell others what you are feeling. You can be more aware of your emotions when looking at these words and perhaps you can find exactly what you are feeling. Are you mad, or filled with rage, or slightly annoyed, or a little bit irritated?

You are the expert on what you're feeling

Nobody else can feel what you're feeling. Nobody else can feel what you are feeling. They might guess at it, but they do not know. You are the only one that knows for sure what your feelings are. You may not yet have the exact words to describe them, but they are real. We can observe our emotions and therefore understand ourselves and others better. Emotions do not have to affect our behavior or the way that we interact with others. Those are choices we get to make.

Emotions can cause us to feel great joy. Emotions can cause us to feel deep pain. Sometimes we wish we could just have the joy and none of the pain. But that is not how life works. In the tapestry of our life, we see only the underside. Dark threads and bright colorful threads are running through this fabric. And yet the pattern is not clear to us. The full richness of the pattern will not be visible until we are with God in heaven. He knows how all this works together and he is making some things beautiful for us. The dark threads outline and cause the colorful threads to shine brighter.

In summary

There is a rich emotional life available for you. It is how God created us. There is a lot of good in the world. There is a lot of beauty in the world even in the midst of struggle. When we look for the beauty in the world, we are moving toward happiness and pleasure. moving towards the restoration of the rich emotional life we are designed to have.

PART TWO

Restoration Of Design In My Head

We talk about what is going on in our head when we actually may mean our mind and thoughts. The second part of *Restoration* is about the way our mind affects our growth and healing or keeps us trapped in wounded places. Our mind helps us to think deeply about life, to process what goes on around us and in us, and to understand each other, and to understand God in deeper and richer ways. When we have been affected by trauma, it can wound our ability to accurately think things through. But restoration and healing are available for you. We are designed to heal.

Do not conform to the pattern of this world, but be transformed by the renewing of your mind. Then you will be able to test and approve what God's will is—his good, pleasing and perfect will.

Romans 12:2

CHAPTER 7

Order out of chaos, Prevention

We are created to be creative, not chaotic. Our minds try to make sense out of what we see, hear, learn, and experience. In the midst of that, we also look at how to bring order out of chaos and try to figure out how to prevent chaos. This calm habit of prevention is not about worrying about things that will or will not happen. Prevention is about objectively thinking, if this happened, what could I do? You make a template in your head for how you would survive, planning how you would move forward. A key skill here is to stop. Once you have identified the concern and planned how to prevent it or survive it to move forward, then you stop thinking about it. This is easier said than done, of course, but let us look at a way to begin this process.

Ten-minute exercise.

Set yourself a timer. Within the allotted ten minutes make four quick lists.

1) You identify the concern. Be as thorough as quickly possible, look at several layers, without having to have all the layers make sense together at this point. Fully write out an objective view of the concern.

2) Then write out the emotional aspect of the concern. All the swirling feelings you have about it. Do not require your feeling to make sense at this point, just record what they are.

3) List out the resources you have to bring to this concern. Include time, skills, other people, ability to research.

4) Write out your desired result. Best case scenario, what do you want?

If you have time left, fill any gaps on the four items.

Now set it all aside and leave it alone for some hours or even a full day. Then come back to it and spend another ten minutes clarifying the list and adding to each section. Again, set it aside and leave it alone for some hours or a day or two. Then you can come back to it, study what you have written, and write out a plan to move forward toward your goals.

What has happened in these ten-minute blocks is that you have begun to bring order to chaos. The swirling thoughts in your brain were written out into a more ordered form. When you did the second ten-minute exercise, you brought even more order to the thoughts.

In the times between focusing on the concern, your brain has been busy in the background working on understanding it more and figuring out how to move forward. No longer stuck trying to remember all the pieces and layers, it was able to make progress.

Your swirling thoughts may have been set in motion by triggers from the past. When you take the time to work through the chaotic thought you are helping to untangle the past triggers from present triggers.

Triggers

A lot of the triggers in our life are set off by our reactions to events in our past. We were wounded and the pain is lingering. What we endured left its mark on us. Our thoughts may feel chaotic and jumbled. The events were in the past, but the effects of it linger in the present. We may wonder why we reacted so strongly to an event now when it was not that big of a deal. It is likely because there is an open wound left from your past that triggered the intense feelings and behaviors in your present.

Journaling is a helpful process of writing down what you are feeling and thinking. You can write down your prayers as well, and the answers to prayers. When you feel a strong reaction to a trigger, writing down whatever is going on within you allows for you to grow in your ability to express what you are feeling and thinking.

I suggest an actual pencil and paper. Writing it on a screen is fine, but there is something visceral about being able to scribble big and hard and large letters by hand that is different than simply putting the words in a 72-point bold font.

If it feels hard to start writing, do it as a ten-minute exercise. Set a timer for ten minutes and write down what is going on for you. Take the full ten minutes, even if you aren't sure what to say next. Write down everything you are thinking and feeling, the things in the present, the things in the past. It does not have to make sense. It does not have to be in full sentences. Then set your journaling aside and walk away to do something else. Take a few moments for good self-care.

Later, when you are feeling, calm you can come back to that and look at what the threads that run through your writing. Was there a time in the past you were feeling the same as the time in the present? What was the same and what was different? What is true and what is not logical? Begin the prevention process of how would you like to respond to that trigger? You can plan out in your mind how you would like your response to be, even write it out and edit it until it feels right. In that process, you are giving your brain a template of how to handle that in the future. It will take a number of times where the trigger reverts to the old pattern, and you intentionally renew this new pattern until eventually, the trigger will go quickly to the new pattern. The journaling process or the reworking of trigger response can be good content you can take to work with your therapist if you have a trusting relationship.

Sometimes a trigger is touched and anger flashes up immediately. Anger is considered a secondary emotion because it is fueled by other emotions. We may feel angry while also feeling vulnerable, threatened, disrespected, or trapped. When you feel angry, observe what else you are feeling and what you are thinking. What does it feel like in your chest and your stomach? What are the thoughts running around in your head? What is the perceived threat you're dealing with? What is the perceived injustice? Observe the anger, but know that your behavior is under your control. You get to choose how you're going to behave when you're angry.

Our anger often has to do with our own values and beliefs. Why get angry when someone disagrees with you? What in their differing opinion makes you feel vulnerable or threatened? When somebody disagrees with you, what is the purpose of getting angry? Why do you need them to agree with you? Everybody is responsible for their own values and their own beliefs. There is freedom for you to have your own values and your own beliefs

Communication issues

Many disagreements between people arise because we are not taking the time to talk through and understand each other. There will be a little irritation and people put up with the annoyance. Not a big deal. But it happens again and again. They put up with it as their annoyance grows. Eventually, they explode in anger over the issue, creating more destruction in the relationship than if they had the courage to have the awkward conversation while the issue was still an annoyance. When you talk through a smaller irritation, it is a low-cost conversation, where you try to deal with something that keeps coming up and put it to rest.

In Summary

We are created to be creative, not chaotic. Our minds try to make sense out of what we see, hear, learn, and experience. In the midst of that, we also look at how to bring order out of chaos and try to figure out how to prevent chaos. This calm habit of prevention includes taking the time to put each small conflict to rest can prevent big conflicts. Also, the skills of polite and kind conflict resolution will help relationships grow stronger. Having an act of calm courage to face awkward conversations can be difficult in the moment, but is an easier life in the long run.

CHAPTER 8

Self talk – Self soothing

Emotions give information that can inform our decisions, but we still need to use our heads and examine the context, so our mind has everything it needs to make good choices. We are given a mind to be able to ponder and think things through, to figure out how to make wise decisions, not decisions that are entirely emotionally driven. The logical way we figure things out is also affected by our self-talk, the story we tell ourselves about events or situations can be used to lower our stress and self-soothe, or it can be used to ramp up our stress and make life harder. That is our choice.

Feeling Anger

Without warning, you feel yourself becoming angry. So far, so good. You are observing your emotions. You have examined the feeling and recognize it as anger.

Now what? Your choice. You can tell yourself you have every right to be angry and replay in your mind every possible perceived wrong you have experienced. As you replay those thoughts, make them welcome, give them a home, and spend time with them, your anger can build to rage that explodes into destructive behavior.

Or you can make a different choice. You can observe your angry feelings and think about what is causing them. Ponder what you want in this situation. Is there something you want changed? Think about the ways that change may affect others, for good or ill. Is the change you want still the best option? Now think through what it would take to get that outcome. Use your feelings of anger to fuel an objective look at the situation from more than your own angle. Identify what the problem is and see the possible paths forward, then move in that direction.

Do not sweat the small stuff

(It is generally all small stuff)

Where thought patterns come from

You can exchange a negative thought pattern for a neutral or positive thought pattern. Before we get to the steps to help change those patterns, let us take a moment to examine where those thought patterns come from. There are a wide variety of sources for your thought patterns. A lot of them started in the environment in which we grew up. We were influenced by the important people in our lives when we were children. Parents, siblings, neighbors, teachers, classmates, and the things we watched and read showed us several different patterns of thinking. We heard people talk and whether they talked about things in a negative, neutral, or positive way, and we took it all in. Over the years and decades, it affected the way that we think about things. At some point, we noticed the positive, neutral, and negative language for what it was. Then we began to choose which way we leaned toward. We always have the choice to just go with the flow, which means thinking in the same type of thought patterns that the people around us are thinking. Or we can choose to reject some of that negativity and make our own considered choices.

Bird making a nest in my hair.

Thoughts and feelings can pop up unexpectedly, triggered by our senses. The meaning we make of all these inputs is informed by our history, our experiences, our beliefs, our thoughts, and our values. The triggers are outside our control. But we have a choice over our thoughts, beliefs, and values. Understand that feelings and thoughts are in some ways like the weather, something triggers them, and we may not have control the fact they show up. But I have control over everything that follows.

It is like the old saying, "I cannot keep a bird from flying over my head, but I can keep it from building a nest in my hair." We may not have much control over thoughts or feelings, but we do not have to make them welcome, spend time with them, and give them a home. We do not have to let them control our behavior, words, or choices. We are responsible for the choices we make, no matter what we are feeling. Just like we are not responsible for other adults' feelings, they are not responsible for our thoughts and feelings.

Weedy field pathways

Another way to visualize the patterns of habits is to imagine a path through a weedy field. There is a solid, well-traveled path that marks your pattern of thinking. It may feel like an easy way or the only way. It is a familiar way that you are used to traveling. The habit of where your thoughts go is reinforced by the things you bring in and spend time with. But it is stressful at times, or it produces thoughts and behavior in you that does not function well in your life, and they leave you feeling stressed or anxious.

You change those old patterns by intentionally choosing to go a different way, like choosing to go another direction in that weedy field. It is hard the first time. It takes extra effort to stomp through the tall weeds and make a new path. You are going to have to walk through the thistles and the tall grass. You fight your way through with effort.

The second time you travel this new path, it is not quite as hard. The third time you go through, it gets a little bit easier. Eventually, that new path becomes as easy to travel as the old one was, and perhaps even easier because you chose a straight direction that reaches your goal sooner.

When you stop traveling the old path, eventually the weeds will re-grow there and make that path more difficult to travel. The new, intentional path you made becomes the easy path. But first, you have to choose to put in the effort and choose to let the old path fill with weeds. As the pattern of choosing the new path becomes stronger, the inclination to take the old path will become less. There will be times you will be busy or distracted and find yourself on the old pathway, but that is a temporary misstep, and you can choose your preferred pathway again.

Perfectionism

Have you ever beat yourself up over not doing something well enough? Do you expect to be able to do some things exactly right? If you got 90% of it done right and the other 10% wrong, do you see the whole thing as a failure? Sounds like you may struggle with perfectionism.

Perfectionism is the need to do things just right, or at least to appear to do things just right. Perfectionism includes the belief that it is possible to do things perfectly. Some people believe that striving to be perfect is a positive trait that is a healthy motivator to constantly get better. But perfection may be an unobtainable goal. If it creates an unreachable goal, that can make you feel unhappy with your life. Excellence may be a better way to define a motivating goal.

Also, I think that depends on whether moving toward the ideal of excellence is a goal to aim toward or a standard to fail against. If you strive for excellence and end up with only very good, that is still a good result. A healthy motivator is a goal to strive toward, not a standard to fail against. By creating smaller goals within the larger goal, you can create ways to succeed along the path toward your goal.

Beating yourself up

Along with perfectionism is the tendency to beat yourself up with self-talk about how lousy you are, how you can never do anything right, how you are a worthless failure. That is exactly the opposite of motivation. Different people are motivated by different things, but very few people are motivated by a constant barrage of negative messages that erode self-worth. People are more often motivated by encouragement of what they did well along with civil and objective discussions of what needs to improve. When you beat yourself up verbally about not being perfect, you could be joining the abusers from your past by sending yourself negative messages about your worth as a human rather than giving objective feedback about your progress in learning a particular skill. One is a rejecting message about self-worth; the other is an encouraging statement about the skill development of a worthy human.

In summary

We were given a mind to be able to ponder and think things through, to figure out how to make wise decisions. Our self-talk, the story we tell ourselves about events or situations, can be used to lower our stress and self-soothe, or it can be used to ramp up our stress and make life harder. That is our choice.

CHAPTER 9

Assertive vs. aggressive

The attitude with which we approach people and tasks can be beneficial or damaging. We get to choose. Assertive communication is direct and respectful. Being calmly assertive gives you the best chance of successfully communicating with others. If you deliver your message in a way that is too passive or too aggressive, the clarity of your message may get lost because people are too busy reacting to the way you delivered it.

Approaching people with an angry, belligerent attitude and showing aggression makes people get ready to defend themselves. Their inner shields go up and they can feel upset and be ready to fight back. When feeling like that, they may not be the least inclined to work with you. If we instead approach people with a strong, calm, polite, and assertive attitude, people are more open and ready to listen. A person with an assertive attitude has a better chance of a positive interaction than a person with an aggressive attitude.

Assertive vs. aggressive

Assertive attitude and body language are bold and confident. It is an attitude of strength under control. It is polite and civil. It can be intense and firm, forceful and insistent. But it is not threatening. When you have an attitude of assertiveness, you are showing equal respect. You respect your own viewpoint, and you also respect the other person's viewpoint or behavior.

An aggressive attitude only respects your own view and not the other person's. Aggressive attitudes and body language are threatening. It is an attitude of strength without control. It can tend toward unprovoked attacks. It seeks to intimidate to get its own way.

How to be assertive without being aggressive

An assertive attitude includes being an active listener: not interrupting when the other person is talking and reflecting on the meaning of what was just said to confirm you heard correctly. Other important aspects of being assertive include:

- Be patient.
- Be prepared.
- Have a confident body posture.
- Make good eye contact.
- Ask for what you want clearly and calmly, speak simply and directly

- Avoid accusing, demeaning or disrespecting the other person.
- Understand and accept differences.
- Stay calm.
- Set appropriate, respectful boundaries.

Fighting Fire

Some people say, "Fight fire with fire." But in cities, we tend to fight fire with water, not more fire. Meeting aggressive behavior with more aggressive behavior tends to escalate the conflict. Some say, "Fight evil with evil," and they justify evil behavior in response to evil behavior. But when we fight evil with evil, evil wins.

It can be like two little kids in a playground. One trips and falls into another one. That one gets mad and shoves back. Then the first one shoves back harder and so it escalates from there and the friendship can be damaged.

Creating safety so you can be heard.

When an argument is carried out with intensity and aggression, it hinders our ability to listen and be heard. It is like we have this full wide capacity to hear and understand to care and have empathy. And yet when are faced with loudness, intensity, and aggression we shut down into a very narrow capacity that is focused primarily on survival.

Functioning in survival mode makes it nearly impossible for us to feel safe enough to figure things out rationally or care about other people. It can feel like we're in a war zone with shells lobbing over our heads. Our analytical understanding is focused on how to survive this minute, how to get to the next safe spot. The caring and compassion part is focused on ducking and running, trying to survive.

If we want to be listened to, we have to create safety in a conversation so people can relax enough that they can access their analytical understanding and caring and compassion parts of the brain. Because of this, creating safety in the conversation is more likely to get you the understanding that you desire.

Healthy assertive communication

Healthy assertive communication includes clearly stating what your concern is, what you would like to have done about it, and why you think your solution is the best option. A calmly assertive attitude gives you a better chance of getting what you want.

Aggression is like burning down your own house to get warm. You get the warmth you wanted—temporarily—but at what cost? When we try to get what we want through aggression, we end up damaging relationships, harming the safety and trust that had been there.

Assertive speech can be polite and direct. Politeness does not mean you do not care about what you are asking about. What it means is you are being respectful to people while you're asking for what you want. You can be calm and yet firm, like a velvet-covered rock.

You also have to look at how important this thing you are asking for is. Is it important enough for you to risk putting some distance or lowered trust in the relationship? What is the deal-breaker for you? Do not fight over small stuff. In life, most of the stuff we argue over it is small stuff. Count the cost.

In summary

An attitude of calm assertiveness will be more likely to build relationships with others, get positive responses to your requests, and make your life easier than an attitude of aggression.

CHAPTER 10

Harmony, Conflict and Anger

When things come together in harmony, it is a pleasing thing for all those involved. Harmony does not mean things have to all be alike. Harmony is when different components work together in a way that is pleasing or beneficial. Conflict is a competitive or opposing difference of ideas or interests. When things are different, or opinions are different it does not mean there has to be conflict. When four singers come together to sing in harmony the beauty of that sound is because of the difference in the notes. If we take the time to seek how the differences could work together everyone can find life easier. Just because people see things differently than we see things is no reason to get angry. Anger is a strong feeling of annoyance, displeasure, or hostility. it can be a secondary emotion in response to other emotions. Often anger is triggered by what we think is going on instead of what actually is.

What we think is going on (clueless, negligent, spiteful)

Often when we get angry it not as much about what is going on as it is about what we think is going on. For example, if I am driving down a busy, four-lane road when a car goes past me and then pulls into my lane a few feet in front of my bumper, I am going to have an emotional reaction. But my reaction is tempered by whatever I think is going on. If the car has a sign on it saying, "student driver, driving school," I think this was clueless. The student who is just learning how to drive had no idea how close he came to causing an accident for both of us. Hopefully, his instructor is letting him know about that right now. I will slow down and give that car more space.

But maybe there is no driving school sign on that car. Perhaps instead what I see is the driver is holding their cell phone up to their ear. They are distracted. This is somebody who is behaving negligently. They did not drive that close to my vehicle on purpose, but they are not doing what an ordinary person would do in that situation because they're distracted. They are not paying close attention to their driving. In this case, I will also slow down and give the driver space, watching out for my own safety, and I may tap my horn to let them know to pay more attention to what they're doing.

But maybe there is no driving school sign, and there is no phone in use. In this scenario, the driver who pulls in front of me looks at me in their rearview mirror, catches my eye, and flips me off with a rude gesture. This is somebody who knows exactly what they're doing. In this case, the driver is spiteful. I will also slow down to get away from this driver because I need to look after my own safety and who knows what they will do next.

Another way to describe this principle is to imagine you are wearing your favorite white shirt. You see a little 2-year-old who loves you dearly and who has just had their peanut butter and grape jelly sandwich. They have grape jelly all over their fingers as they come running over to give you a big hug. That child has no idea what grape jelly does to a white shirt. They are clueless.

Now contrast it to having lunch with your friend and your friend is excitedly telling you about their wonderful trip. They are using arm gestures and they knock their grape soda off of the table and onto your white shirt. This was negligent. They did not mean to; it was an accident. But you still have grape stains on your white shirt.

The third example is when somebody is near you, they have a glassful of grape soda. They look you right in the eyes and they splash it all over you. This was spiteful.

In all three of these scenarios, you have a grape stain on your white shirt. Yet our emotional response may be different in each of these situations. It would be unkind to be mad at a toddler who loves you. This was clueless behavior. We tend to teach clueless people about their behavior. There is no reason to get mad. It is just clueless, and they need education and training.

For our negligent friend, we move their glass to a safer spot, with a gentle reminder to be careful. With someone who is spiteful, we need to protect ourselves from this threat to our safety.

- Clueless people we educate, teach, and train.
- Negligent people we remind.
- Spiteful people, we avoid, protecting our own safety.

However, often when a person does something that hurts us, we immediately jump to the conclusion that it was spiteful. We get angry at the perceived threat or the disrespect. When we constantly assume that everyone and every action is spiteful, we end up living in a world that feels difficult and threatening. If on the other hand, we assume good motives to start with and that perhaps people are just clueless or doing the best they know how our world would feel less stressful.

We can view our differences as less stressful if we see them as appropriate harmony. Harmony is things that go well together even though they are different. An example of this is a barbershop quartet, where four people sing together. Even though their voices are different, and they sing different notes, there is a beautiful harmony of sound. When we accept that the richness of humankind is within the differences and that those very differences are what can produce harmony we have moved into a better world. To live in harmony is not to be the same as others or have them agree with you. Harmony is about being different and yet working well together. When we respect ourselves and others we can accept their differences and seek how we can work together, live together in harmony. Making life better for everyone.

Feeling anger is not wrong

"In your anger do not sin": Do not let the sun go down while you are still angry,
Ephesians 4:26

This passage expects us to have feelings of anger, but also assumes that our thoughts and behavior are under our control and that we can choose to end our anger. Anger is a feeling that may lash up in response to a perceived injustice, a perceived threat. It is normal to have feelings of anger. However, when we feel angry, we are responsible for our response, our thoughts, and our behavior. We make choices about how we will handle it, and we get to deal with the consequences of our behavior. If we choose to react in a hostile or violent way and destroy things or hurt people, we are responsible for all that we do. Feeling angry is no excuse for behaving badly. Your behavior is still your choice.

Fighting fair.

When a couple argues, the dysfunctional and unfair way people fight is to be loud, aggressive, and intimidating. They say words designed to hurt deeply. They bring up everything from the past and generalize saying things like you always, you never. The result of this kind of dysfunctional fighting is that relationships get damaged. Sometimes beyond repair. People may feel threatened. Feelings of safety and trust are broken.

The healthy way to deal with conflict is to fight fair. Keep your volume and tone civil and respectful. Do not say anything to damage or hurt someone's heart. Stick to the single matter at hand. Explain what you see the problem is as objectively as possible. Listen to and encourage the other person to explain their point of view on the topic. Rephrase and say their statement back to them in other words showing that you understand them to mean about their viewpoint. Then when the problem is defined, start together to think about ways to resolve the concern so this issue can be put to rest, so you can live in harmony.

A tale of two families

These two families are the same. Same ethnic background, same economic situation, they even live next door to each other. Everything the same. Except. In Family A when there is an argument, no matter how long it takes, they talk through problems. In Family B when there is an argument, everyone separates and goes to their own space to calm down. Maybe later they will come back and discuss it.

Neither of these is right nor wrong, just a different culture surrounding how to handle disagreements. But what happens when the children grow up and the boy from Family A marries the girl from Family B? They have their first argument. One tries to stay and talk, and one tries to go away and cool down, but the other keeps following and will not leave her alone. Then they also start arguing about not being loved or respected, when what they really mean is, "You are not handling arguments in the way I am used to." Both are trying their hardest to respectfully handle arguments as they were handled in the culture in which they grew up.

Fighting fair requires that when someone feels too emotionally activated to discuss the concerns, they step away and cool down. That only works if the other party will give them time and space. So, the one who wants to step away says something like, "I need to take a time out here. I will come back and discuss with you later." They set a time, and the other one needs to respect that and give them time.

The challenge here is why does the person want to let them step away if they are afraid that they will never come back to finish the discussion? And why would the person who is stepping away want to bring it up again when they fear it will just start the whole argument over again? The challenge here is that both have to take the risk of letting someone step away and calm down, and the risk and coming back to discuss the concerns when both are calmer. Both people need to work toward being gentle and understanding while retraining their conflict habits.

Stepping away to cool down is only a part of healthy, fair fighting. Another important part is to listen until you hear the other person out fully. Ask these types of questions: Why is this an issue for you? What else is involved in it? How are you affected by it? Seek to fully understand before you present your side. Understanding someone else's point of view does not mean you agree with it. You can fully understand and still disagree. Those are two different things. After one side feels like they have been heard and understood, it is their turn to listen and seek to understand the other side. Both sides need to be able to fully present their sides.

The next step is about assumptions and goals. In my counseling practice, when couples argue, I encourage them to remember this basic assumption: *my spouse loves me and respects me.* That underlying assumption—verbally validated now and then—helps us to see the concern in a clearer light. Some deal-breaking concerns will break up a couple, but most are not deal-breakers; they are annoyances that can erode the happiness out of a relationship if not dealt with and resolved. Resolving or putting to rest an issue prevents you from having to argue about the same things over and over.

Our right to say no and deal with the consequences.

At times, we may feel anger when other people do not handle things the same way as we would, or they do not believe like us, or they do not behave like us. We may think they are wrong simply because they make different choices than we would.

When you feel like something is wrong, it is good to stop and ask yourself, "Why is it wrong? Wrong according to what standard?"

- Is it wrong according to a legal standard?
- Is it wrong according to a moral standard?
- Is it wrong according to a biblical standard?
- Is it wrong according to an ethical standard? Which one?
- Is it wrong according to a standard of competency?

- Is it wrong according to a personal preference standard?

For example, if the window glass gets washed and it has streaks left all over it, we would say that the window was washed wrong. But it is not illegal to leave streaks on a window. It is not immoral to leave streaks on the glass. The Bible does not discuss the washing of window glass. It is not unethical to leave streaks on the glass. But according to the professional competency standards of window washing, leaving streaks is wrong. Perhaps it is also wrong according to personal preference.

Some things we may think are wrong are only personal preferences. For instance, if I say that I think a sofa should be blue and you think a sofa should be green, there is nothing illegal or immoral or even incompetent about choosing the color of the sofa. That is a personal preference. Having a personal preference regarding to my own stuff is fine. But a wrong happens when we try to force our personal preference on others. I tell you that all sofas need to be blue, and you say that all sofas need to be green. Now we are arguing who is right and who is wrong.

When we feel like something is wrong, we need to check ourselves first. If it is a personal preference wrong, we do not get to tell other people what to do with their own lives. People can get intensely emotional about their opinions of what is right and wrong.

Unity, not uniformity

The biblical standard is that we, as Christian brothers and sisters serving Christ, live as part of one body. We have unity in our purpose and our goal to worship God. The differences between us enhance the whole.

So, the body is not made up of just one part.
It has many parts.
1 Corinthians 1:14

This passage points out that we need to embrace the differences we have. Be aware of the ways that differences provide harmony. Look for ways we can have unity, but don't try to force everyone to be uniform. Harmony brings beauty and richness to life. Trying to control others to be just like you, to do things like you do things can lead to anger and conflict.

Anger is a normal part of life. When we see others being hurt or abused when we experience injustice anger may be an ordinary response. But out-of-control anger can destroy. But there are healthy and unhealthy ways to deal with anger.

Healthy ways to deal with anger

- Observe—Start by just observing when anger is triggered. You can prevent a lot of anger by looking at the things that trigger anger inside of you and deciding whether those are healthy or not. Then work to resolve the old anger triggers.
- Self-Control—Feeling anger is okay, a common human emotion. But everything that follows

you have control over. You are responsible for your thoughts and your actions.

- Express—You can let people know you are angry by clearly stating, "I am feeling upset and angry about that." Tell them politely and respectfully why you are upset and what you would like to see done about the issue.
- Accept—We do not always get what we want. Accepting that makes life less stressful.

Unhealthy ways to express anger

- Lash out with disrespectful words that attack a person's character or value.
- Violent behavior or words.
- Destruction of property, such as slamming doors or breaking things.
- Threatening words, posture, or behavior.
- Coercing or manipulating words or behavior.

Some people have the illusion that all anger is a display of strength. In self-controlled anger, there can be a strength when feelings of anger are used to do something positive. Unhealthy anger destroys and tears down. Unhealthy anger often comes not out of strength, but out of weakness and fear.

However, there is a force in the world that is stronger than anger. As we discussed in chapter one, the strongest force in the world is love. People will do things for love they would not do because they are angry. The power of love is the strongest force for change in the world.

And now these three remain:
faith, hope and, love.
But the greatest of these is love.
1 Corinthians 13:13

In summary

To live in harmony is a healthy part of life. It makes everyone's life better. To have harmony is not about being the same as others or have them agree with you. Harmony is about being different and yet working well together. When we respect ourselves and others, we can accept their differences and seek how we can work and live together in harmony, making life better for everyone.

CHAPTER 11

Forgiveness

Forgiveness is an important part of restoration. When we forgive others, we are released from the pain of resentment. We clean the bitterness out of our own heart. We move toward a healthy life when we forgive others. We also move toward a healthy life when we ask others to forgive us. Sometimes forgiveness feels hard. Either direction—to give forgiveness or to receive forgiveness. In this chapter, we will examine what is involved with forgiveness and some parallel concepts as well.

When we think of forgiveness, we sometimes mix different concepts together. When considering the act of forgiveness, it is helpful to look at each of these concepts separately.

- **Forgiveness** is when our wrong is pardoned. We no longer have it held against us, although there may still be consequences to deal with.
- **Reconciliation** is the process of two people who have been in conflict agreeing to make amends or come to a place of being able to be in a relationship again.
- **Trust** is an attitude toward another individual, a confident hope or a firm belief in the character, strength, or truth of someone.
- **Forgetting** is to stop thinking about, put out of one's mind. When a memory of a past experience is no longer thought of or considered.
- **Safety** is about not continuing to be in danger from the one who hurt us.

We can forgive the abuser and still not want to be around him again. We can forgive an abuser and still not let her be around our children. We can choose to forgive even if we cannot forget. We can choose to forgive even when reconciliation is not possible. We can choose to forgive and still keep ourselves safe.

Forgiveness and trust

If I walk into the room and step on your foot as I go by, would you forgive me? Most people would forgive an accident. But the next time I walk into the room, where are your feet? Likely you will have them tucked safely under your chair, away from my feet. Does that mean you did not forgive me? No. What it means is I broke trust. Even though you have forgiven me, it may take ten times of me walking by and you seeing that I am intentionally being careful to not hurt you before you begin to trust me again.

But what happens if I have carefully walked by six times and then step on your foot again? Now it may take a hundred times of you seeing that I am being careful before you trust me again. If I go about 80 times and then step on you again, now it may take a thousand times of me being careful before that original level of trust returns. Trust rebuilding is possible, but it takes time. This is exponentially true if someone continues to break trust.

What happens if I step on your foot and you say, "I forgive you," and I get mad? "What are you forgiving me for? It was your fault for having your foot in the way." Where is trust in that scenario? It is shattered. The thing about forgiveness is that we have to own our wrongdoing if it is of any value to us. If I deny that I have done wrong, I do not want your forgiveness, because your forgiveness feels like an accusation of wrongdoing. There would be no trust and no safety in that situation.

There are two directions of forgiveness: giving forgiveness and receiving forgiveness. In our Christian heritage, our forgiveness was provided for on the cross. Christ died in our place for all the wrongs we have done.

For all have sinned and fall short of the glory of God
Romans 3:23

Is this forgiveness available to all people? Yes. But are all the people in the world forgiven? No. That forgiveness does not do them any good until they agree with God that they have done wrong and need forgiveness.

If we confess our sins, he is faithful and just
and will forgive us our sins and
purify us from all unrighteousness.
1 John 1:9

There are conditions to receiving forgiveness. This passage says "IF" we confess, he is faithful and just to forgive us. That 'if' is about agreeing with God that we have offended. That forgiveness is freely available to us. God is ready and willing to forgive.

When people have wronged us, we have the choice to decide to forgive and work through the process of forgiving. That is a work in our hearts between us and God. Since we have been forgiven we can forgive. If we choose not to forgive it may hinder our own relationship with God, and it keeps us trapped in pain. Forgiving can release us from the pain and the chains of the old wounds and let us move forward unhindered by the resentments of the past. But our offer of forgiveness does not do the offender any good until they agree that they have offended and accept our forgiveness.

For if you forgive other people when they sin against
you, your heavenly Father will also forgive you. But if
you do not forgive others their sins, your Father will
not forgive your sins.

Matthew 6:14-15

God's command to forgive is pretty clear, and we are not commanded to do something impossible. Choosing to forgive is a decision of will; it does not depend upon feelings. We can forgive while we still feel pain, while we still hurt, while we are still dealing with the consequences of someone else's behavior. When we choose to forgive, it may not be easy. It may not be fast. It does not fix everything.

Choosing to forgive is a decision, but the process of forgiving may take time. We may wake up every morning still feeling the hurt and the resentment trying to invade our lives. But we can remind ourselves, "No, I have chosen to forgive this. God, please help me to keep on this path of forgiving." Forgiveness is a choice, and then a process, a decision first and later a feeling. Our feelings will eventually come in line with our decisions. It may take a long time and we may have to remind ourselves daily that we have chosen to forgive, but our feelings will eventually follow, and the hurt will eventually fade.

When we have done wrong and we go to God and ask for forgiveness, God freely gives it to us. When we have wronged another person and we go to that person and humbly ask for forgiveness, they may or may not give it to us. But our healing is not based on their response. Our healing is based on the work in our own heart before God. We are not held hostage waiting for another human to forgive us. They may be in their own healing process and not yet be ready to give forgiveness.

Sometimes people say, "I have asked God for forgiveness, and I do not feel forgiven." But remember: forgiveness is not based on a feeling. God promises us in his word that he will forgive us when we ask him.

We can rely on that promise. When those unforgiven feelings come up, remind yourself of that promise.

Sometimes we do not feel forgiven because we are not the one guilty of the offense. Only the one guilty of the offense benefits from the forgiveness of that guilt. Others may feel bad that the event happened and know that there is guilt, and that forgiveness is needed in the situation. But who needs to confess the guilt and who needs to be forgiven?

Forgiveness and justice

Sometimes we can get caught up in wanting justice. We may not want to forgive because then we feel like the offender has gotten away with bad behavior with no consequences. What does God require of us?

> *He has shown you, O mortal, what is good.*
> *And what does the Lord require of you?*
> *To act justly and to love mercy*
> *and to walk humbly with your God.*
> *Micah 6:8*

To act justly, to love mercy, and to walk humbly. To act justly means that I need to do the next right thing, that I focus on the justice I am giving and doing, not focus on the justice or injustice being done to me. To love mercy is to be kind and merciful to others, giving them grace, undeserved favor. And to walk humbly before our God is to recognize our own need for mercy and to be grateful to God for his great loving kindness to us.

Some people get stuck on wanting—even demanding—justice. But the world is not just. Not fair. When you have two items and I only have one, there is in me a part that wants to cry out, "That is not fair! That is not just!" And yet when I have two items and you have one, that same part of me may not seem to be so concerned with justice. When we strive to be treated fairly, we may be unjust to someone else in the process. We may need to ask ourselves, "Do you really want all that you have coming to you?" Think of all the wrongs you have done in life. Have you been punished for each and every one, big and small? Do you really want what you have coming to you? Myself, I do not want justice. I want mercy. I crave mercy.

In summary

Forgiveness is an important part of restoration. We move toward a healthy life when we forgive others and ask others to forgive us. Sometimes forgiveness feels hard. Either direction—to give forgiveness or to receive forgiveness. But forgiveness is a choice of will, and is not dependent on feelings.

CHAPTER 12

_____

Acceptance and submission

Why did this happen? Why to me? Why now?

Sometimes life is not to our liking; we cannot have what we want. Life is not fair. Life is not easy. We wonder why everyone else has it easier and I have to deal with a hard life. First off, let us look at that statement: "Everyone else has it easier." How do you know everyone else has it easier? If you pay attention to other people you may find that everyone struggles with some aspects of life. Parts of life you have easy may be difficult for others. The part you find hard may be easy for others.

We ask for what we think we want; we pray and earnestly seek. Sometimes we ask for something at home or at work and the answer is "No." We see no reason for the negative answer, so we ask again. We give it our best argument. And the answer is still no.

At that point, we have to make a decision. Are we going to sneak around and try to get our own way by deceit or defy the no outright and try to force our own way? Either of those will damage the relationship and your own character. Or are we going to respect the no even though we do not agree with it? To accept the no and respectfully submit does not necessarily mean we agree. At times, what we want seems like it would be good for us, even something we need. But we cannot get it. The answer seems to be "no". No matter how we ask, we cannot get it. Understand that the answer is not about your worth as a human being, it is about this one request. It is not about your value.

When we practice radical acceptance, we stop fighting against reality, stop throwing tantrums, and stop responding with impulsive or destructive behaviors when things are not going how we wanted. In radical acceptance, we let go of the bitterness that can keep us trapped in a cycle of disappointment and suffering.

To accept the current reality is NOT approval, but rather choosing to accept that we cannot change the facts. They are out of our control. When we do this, we stop ourselves from getting trapped in unhappiness, bitterness, and anger. We stop unnecessary suffering.

We can choose to accept what we cannot change. The important next step is to stop deciding. Do not ask yourself every day if you are going to accept this, just do it. It is like accepting the weather. If we spend energy railing against the rain, the rain is not going to go away. Railing against things that we cannot change is a waste of energy, the rain will not care if we rail. We will just feel frustrated. If we accept that it rains, then we will adapt to reality and wear protective rain gear to keep us comfortable in the rain. It does not take any energy; it is neutral. We will just look at it and neutrally say, "Oh it is raining today," put on our rain gear and go on about life.

When there is a loss we need to accept, we need to let ourselves grieve the loss of hopes, then go on to look for the next thing. Do not let the loss of the past hopes steal away the hopes in your future. There is a place and a time for lamenting the loss. Then, choose to accept this loss and look forward to what could be out there for you.

A Time for Everything

There is a time for everything,
and a season for every activity under the heavens:
a time to be born and a time to die,
a time to plant and a time to uproot,
a time to kill and a time to heal,
a time to tear down and a time to build,
a time to weep and a time to laugh,
a time to mourn and a time to dance,
a time to scatter stones and a time to gather them,
a time to embrace and a time to refrain from
embracing,
a time to search and a time to give up,
a time to keep and a time to throw away,
a time to tear and a time to mend,
a time to be silent and a time to speak,
a time to love and a time to hate,
a time for war and a time for peace.
Ecclesiastes 3:1-8

When we accept what we cannot change, we are releasing ourselves from the destructive habits of bitterness and anger. It is a part of maturing into abundant life. The future is unknown to us, but not to God. He knows where you are and what is going on in your life as well as what will happen later. When you have accepted your current state, you have freed yourself to look into the future toward the blessings God has in store.

When the loss is because of a negative decision of someone in control, an authority, the decision to accept the no" is submission to governing authorities. Submission, in this case, is not a passive act of a weak person; it can be the conscious choice of someone who is strong and chooses to be obedient to God and to the governing authority.

Let everyone be subject to the governing authorities, for there is no authority except that which God has established.The authorities that exist have been established by God.
Romans 13:1

Sometimes there are some negative choices a ruling authority may make that we choose not to submit to so we can obey God rather than man.

When we accept what we do not have the power to change and submit to the things we would like to change but it is not in our authority to change, we are choosing to submit. In that acceptance and submission, we find peace. Jesus submitted to death. Submit to God and trust that he still loves you in the midst of trouble.

In Summary

Sometimes we cannot have what we want, and life is not to our liking. The truth is that life is not fair. Life is not easy. Everyone struggles with some aspects of life. The parts of life you have easy may be difficult for others. Part you find hard may be easy for others. There are seasons in life that are harder than others. When we learn to accept what we cannot change, there is less misery. God still loves you in the midst of trouble.

PART THREE

Restoration Of Design In Growth And Healing

We are designed to grow and to heal. The first part of *Restoration* is about the wide range of emotions we are designed to feel as human beings. The second part is about how we think and process in our minds. This third part is about the choices we make and working through the process of growth and healing. Restoration and healing are available for you. We are designed to heal.

CHAPTER 13

Courage

It is a hard job to look at the past and heal from childhood wounds. It takes a lot of courage. Some people have spent all their time up until now pushing that pain away, not looking at it and trying to numb it. We have figured out how to survive, even if we are being hindered by the past.

The wounds of the past have difficulty healing if they still have foreign objects embedded. Think of it as a sliver. When we get a sliver in our finger, sometimes it goes in so deep not all of it can easily be removed. It may heal up over the top of the sliver. It is no longer bleeding, but it is not fully healed, either.

The only way for those wounds to fully heal is to reopen the wound and dig out the splinter. That is going to hurt more than leaving a splinter in for a little while. Right now, the splinter may only hurt when we bang it into something. If we do not bang it, we are not aware that it is there. It is a little red, sore, and maybe a little infected, but it is not causing a lot of trouble—if we are careful to not use that finger.

We feel like it is only hindering us a little. But the infection is still there, and it is not healing. Deciding that you are going to look at what's going on with it, poke around it and open it up and let the pus drain out of it, then dig around for the sliver still inside, takes courage.

We figured out how to cope with our abuse in our childhood. The coping skills we used as a child were healthy coping skills for that time, in that place. Coping is a part of our resilience. But the thing about those childhood coping skills is they are like the milk in our refrigerator: they have an expiration date. When they get past the expiration date, they turn into something else. The coping skills that were healthy and helped you to survive the abuse as a child can cripple your growth and healing as an adult. They can keep you isolated and alone or keep you making wrong decisions based on fear, not wanting to bump that old wound and not knowing how to keep it from hurting.

When we decide it's time for healing, then it takes a lot of courage to look at how ugly those wounds are. Courage to remember the betrayals of your childhood, not just the betrayal by the abuser but also the betrayal of those who should have protected you and did not, those who should have known you were in pain and should have helped you and did not. Perhaps the very ones who abused you might have been among those who should have protected you.

For us to take a look at how helpless we were as a child and see how much we should have been protected can be eye-opening. Look around at children that are the age that you were when you were first abused. Look at how vulnerable they are, how easy they are to manipulate, how powerless. And yet you survived that trauma. The fact that we can survive trauma abuse shows that we have resilience and strength.

Now we need a different kind of strength to look at the wounds and heal. We have these trauma memories that have both an emotional component and a mental component. The wounds are often focused on the emotional component and the objective, logical part of the memory may be incomplete. To heal, we need to look at the memories not just emotionally but also objectively. It can be helpful to write a description of what went on. Sometimes that is intensely emotional and impactful, and you might want to do it in a therapy session with a mental health therapist.

Write out first just the objective facts. For example, A 7-year-old girl is in a bedroom of an apartment. A 35-year-old man, her stepfather, comes into the room and exposes his private parts, telling the girl she has to rub his private parts. She feels uneasy and scared. A 28-year-old woman, her mother, is in the kitchen cooking dinner. That is an objective description of what went on.

When you look at that memory, maybe with your therapist by your side, ask yourself, "What does the law say about the event?" That is an illegal act. "Who is to blame for that act?" It is not the 7-year-old child. The 35-year-old man may tell the 7-year-old she is the one that are responsible for what went on, but that is a lie, another part of the abuse.

Now as an adult you can see that 7-year-old children have no responsibility for what went on in that room. Look at how vulnerable such young children are and how easily manipulated. What happened to a child who suffered abuse is not the child's fault. However, it is our responsibility what kind of adult we become.

If you are in a safe support group, ask what are the other people in that support group think about the activity that went on in that room and who was at fault. Ask what your therapist thinks about it. It helps you to get a more objective view when you can find out that it is not just you who thinks it was wrong, and the adult was to blame. There is a normalization that happens when you finally risk telling about these events out loud, in a safe place. It is important to first do this in a safe place, whether that is a safe support group or safe in the sessions with your mental health therapist. It can be healing to finally be able to say it out loud. The silence of abuse is part of what has been keeping you trapped. Silence is what the abuser usually demands, and silence is for the benefit of the abuser. Silence allows them to continue to abuse.

Expect to feel an emotional response when you start looking at how you were betrayed, how were you were abused, and how you were treated when you were vulnerable and powerless. There may be sadness, shock, anger, and some depression. A time when you need to grieve. It is okay to feel whatever you feel. Being able to grieve and cry about the wounds of the past can help to wash them clean in our memory. You now know that yes, we were hurt, we were damaged. Your therapist can help you healthily work through these.

The damage of abuse often lingers into our adulthood. It can affect the way we trust people or not, the way that we interact with others, the way that we want to be around lots of others, or the way that we want to be alone. All of that can be affected by what happened to us as a child or in domestic violence as an abused partner. It takes courage to face these old wounds.

Courage is not the absence of fear; it is feeling fear and yet going on. There is a story about a boy and his dog. The boy falls through thin ice on a creek, and he is stuck in the icy water. He does not have the strength to get himself out of the creek and he is scared as he hangs on to an old tree branch. He does not know how long he can hang on in that icy water. The dog runs back to get help. The boy keeps repeating to himself, "Courage consists in holding on one moment longer. Courage consists in holding on one moment longer." And he can hold on till help comes.

Courage is holding on one minute longer.

When we are working through some of the wounds of the past, it takes courage just to sit with that discomfort and not push it away or use a substance to try to numb it out. It takes courage to be able to sit with that discomfort for one moment longer and grieve. Then take time to be compassionate to yourself. Think about when you were a child. What did you need a comforting adult to do or to say for you then? Can you say those words for yourself now? It is like the adult you are is comforting the child you were, saying it is going to be alright, you are going to survive this, life will be better in the future. It takes courage to objectively look at the wounds of the past and see the truth of them.

Truth is healing
and perhaps awkward, messy, and uncomfortable,
but tremendously good.

In Summary

When it's time for healing, then it takes a lot of courage to look at the wounds of the past. For us to take a look at how helpless we were as a child and see how much we should have been protected can be hard to consider. And yet you survived that trauma. The fact that we can survive trauma abuse shows that we have courage.

CHAPTER 14

Resolving, Putting the Past to Rest

We do not have to stay hindered by the pain of the past. We can put in the hard work of putting the past to rest. Examining the wounds and touching them with healing. Answering fearful, hurtful lingered thoughts with truth and peace. This will help us be freed from past trauma.

Worldview

Our values, beliefs, and opinions fuel our feelings. Values give us information and help us in the decisions that we make, and our beliefs inform that process. When we have been abused, though, our beliefs may have been damaged. Our worldview can grow lopsided. We may believe that we are shameful, that no one will love us because of the way we've been hurt and damaged. That belief is wrong. As an abused child grows up, their view of the world and their own value and their place in the world can be distorted by the trauma they endure. It is good as an adult to take another look at why we believe what we believe. Where does it come from? Is it true? Do I still believe it, or do I need to look at it layer by layer to sort out truth from distortion?

One little girl looked around at her world and she saw that daddy put his teeth in a glass at night. Mommy did not do that. Her older brothers did not do that. She made sense of her world by saying to herself, "Adult males end up putting their teeth in the glass at night, but adult females did not do that and that must be the way that the world works." While she had observed her world and saw the pieces that were in it, her conclusion was wrong. It was a childish conclusion. Without her having said that to anybody, she grew up with that view in the back of her mind. Later, as she became an adult, she understood that childish conclusion was wrong. She examined the truth and corrected her belief.

As an abused child or someone who is in midst of domestic violence, there can be a number of distorted beliefs. The victim looks around at how the world is and may believe that all relationships are like this one. That her value is less than the value of the abuser. That she has no power to change the situation. That there is no other type of situation in the world, they are all like this, so make the best of it.

These distorted beliefs can linger even after the victim is out of the situation and safe, growing, and healing. A faint doubt can linger that no one will love her for who she is, that she is too damaged to be happy. That the abuser is the only one who wants her at all. Abusers want the victim to believe that this is the normal way of life and that is part of the lie. It is part of the worldview that is wrong.

In order to put the past to rest, it is good to examine your beliefs and your values. When you feel sad or of less value, write down what you are feeling and thinking. Set that aside until you are feeling better. Then take a look at the things you thought and believed. Examine which of those things are true and which of those things were a distorted part of that abusive life.

In order to live a healthy life, we need to know what we what a healthy life looks like. Look around at the lives you see. Look for older people who seem happy and confident. What is their life like? How do they treat others? How do they treat family? Sometimes we can struggle to see how to move forward. It can be helpful to explore these ideas with a mental health counselor who can help you see your past more objectively and help you process old wounds to move toward health and healing. Through counseling, your mental health therapist can help you see a more objective view of your past and guide you as you move into a healthy way of living.

Turning the garbage of life into fertile soil for new growth: a metaphor describing the counseling process.

In life, we have garbage. In this metaphor, there is no landfill and no garbage pickup service. So, life hands us garbage, or we go out and get garbage, or garbage is dumped on our doorstep through no fault of our own. What should we do with it? Often, we toss it into a closet, or a corner of the garage and pull the door shut. There. Now that everything is out of sight, it is just fine. Another load comes, so we throw that in the garage, too.

We get pretty good at keeping our doorstep and driveway clear. But eventually, a black, sticky, smelly mess oozes out from under the garage door. It affects our daily life. We walk around it, but it spreads more and more. Other people notice it. It sticks to our shoes; it gets tracked into every part of our world. So, we get busy, clean up the mess, and scrub down the driveway. Sometimes we need help with the driveway cleaning; sometimes we can do it by ourselves. Once the driveway is clean, things are going well again. But the sticky, smelly ooze keeps coming back, because the source is still there. Time alone does not take care of this kind of problem.

What a mental health therapist does in counseling is help clients clean up the driveway and, if they want, that counselor will help them deal with the source and clean up the garage too. Therapists have worked with a lot of smelly garages, and they know how to help.

So, what can be done with all that garbage?

It can be composted!

Turning the refuse of life into fertile soil for new growth.

In the garden, composting is how you turn the refuse of life into fertile soil for new growth. In mental health therapy, you talk through the traumas and struggles of life, putting the past to rest and turning it into fertile ground for new growth.

Dealing with old matter

- In the garden—Add carbon-rich matter like Dead leaves, decaying matter, fertilizer
- In therapy—What happened in your past

Dealing with fresh new matter

- In the garden—Add nitrogen or protein-rich matter like: lawn clippings, garbage
- In therapy—What is going on now, today

Air circulation

- In the garden— Stack the pile in a way that there is adequate oxygen
- In therapy—Talk about these things with a therapist

Heat is generated

- In the garden—The composting process may generate its own heat
- In therapy—There may be angry feelings to deal with

Moisture applied

- In the garden— Keep compost moist. Water occasionally, or let the rain do the job
- In therapy—Perhaps a time to grieve, or cry

Turning the pile appropriately

- In the garden— give the pile a quick turn to aerates the pile

- In therapy—Professional direction for insight

If this composting, growth, and healing process is treated in the right way, with the right mixture, the result turns that huge pile of smelly, sticky, messy garbage into a rich resource of composted soil, ready for new growth. (Done wrong, it remains a big troublesome pile).

Among the hindrances to resolving the past is a reluctance to dig up all that painful stuff. We want to believe it is in the past, done and gone. But although the original events were in the past, the lingering effects are in the present. Resolving the past can be hindered by other people in the extended family who want to keep silent; they do not want to think about it anymore. They want to say all the past is in the past, which is true, but the effects of the past are in the present. The pain and sadness can linger in the present. If we want our present and our future to be healthy and free of the past, we need to deal with the messy work of putting the past to rest.

Healing exercises

One of the exercises people find helpful is to think about one event in their past—not the worst, most painful one, but one of the smaller, less impactful ones. Then write out letters, but NOT letters you are going to send to anyone. This is an exercise you are writing out for your own growth. Write out what you would have liked to have said to the person who abused you. Write what you would like to have said to those who could have protected you and did not. State objectively what you experienced, what their behavior was then, the effect it had on you at the time, and the effect it is still having on you now. What you are writing is for yourself, so you fully understand the impact this has had on your life. I suggest writing it with pencil and paper. If you feel anger, you can scribble boldly and large. If you are sad you can write small and faint. DO NOT SEND these letters. This is only the first part of this healing exercise. It can be very helpful to work through this with a counselor.

The next step is to set it aside and let it rest for days or weeks. Later, you can come back to the letters and edit them to explain more clearly and objectively what you experienced. When it feels like a more finished version, now may be the time to do the empty chair exercise. This is best done with your therapist.

Set up an empty chair. Sit in a chair across from it. Imagine the person the letter is to is sitting in that chair. Read the letter out loud as if they were there. Take time to feel what you are feeling. If there's anger there, express it. If there is grief, let it out. In a safe place with your therapist, you can deal with the emotions and let some of the pain out, moving that trauma toward healing. Let some part of the past be resolved. Afterward, comfort yourself and do some self-care. Take time to write down what this exercise was like for you.

Journaling

Writing out what you are thinking, and feeling is a helpful way to process your healing. When you have a safe place and a safe way to write it where nobody else is going to read it, you can write exactly what you are feeling thinking. It does not have to make sense; it does not have to be in full sentences. It can even be in pictures or colors. Whatever it takes to express yourself. When you are mad and upset, just splat it all down there. Express exactly what you are feeling. When you are sad and grieving, write that down.

Later, when you are feeling calm, you can look over what you expressed and look for truth and distortions, look for threads of insight and understanding. Look at it and see the wounds, what is not accurate in worldview, what lies of the past are still crippling you, and where you have the truth. Then write out again your new understanding of the healing step you just went through. In that way, you can process a little bit more and then move forward. The goal is to put this part to rest so it does not torment you anymore. So it does not cripple your future anymore. So it does not make you suffer in the present anymore.

Three more vital steps to putting the past to rest are repair, acceptance, and forgiveness.

- Repair—looking at where my behavior has hurt others, seeking to acknowledge what I have done. Seeking God's forgiveness, and then seeking forgiveness from those I have hurt.
- Acceptance—knowing that I cannot change the past. What was done to me in the past may not have been my fault, but I am fully responsible for the kind of adult I have become. Accept what has happened and move forward.
- Forgiving others—acknowledging what was done against you. Seeing the full truth of it. Then choosing to forgive the offender. Choosing to forgive is a choice of will. Afterward comes the work of the forgiving process. Our feelings

may lag behind our choices. Forgiveness frees us from pain and resentment.

In Summary

You cannot change the past. But you can keep the past from crippling your future. God is your healer, and he can bring you healing in many different ways. Healing is often awkward, messy, and uncomfortable, but always very good.

CHAPTER 15

Grace and Value

Grace is unmerited favor. Unmerited means there is nothing we did to earn this favor, this kindness. Grace is freely given to us by God. Grace is about not being afraid. Your life can be filled with confidence every day, knowing that God loves you. There is nothing you can do to lose that love. We can be angry, upset, and frustrated. We can fail and fall, make mistakes big and small. We are still loved. We may struggle with doing the right thing, but we are forgiven. As we have been forgiven, we forgive others. As we have freely received grace, we give grace to others.

God loves us, and his Word tells us how to live. When we miss that mark, make mistakes, and fail, there are consequences as he guides us back into how we should live. But he always loves us. His love is not conditional on us obeying him first and then he will love us. No, we are secure in his love, to live in love and good deeds. You are free to be different, to be vulnerable, to speak the truth.

Living in grace includes obedience, respect, boundaries, and discipline. We have a lot of space within God's clear moral boundaries to make choices of how we want to live. God loves diversity and variety as evidenced by nature all around us. You have value, you are secure in God's love; go make a positive difference in the world.

We have inherent value just because we exist. Our value does not rely on anything we do or do not do or on anything done to us. The value human beings have is just because we exist. Think about a newborn baby, holding the tiny child in your arms. Does that baby have value? Of course, it does. Yet all that baby does is swallow and eliminate. We understand the baby has value just because they exist, just because they are human.

Can we lose that core value? No, we never lose that value since that value does not rely on anything that we do or do not do or anything that happened to us or did not happen to us. We are valuable and worthy of dignity and respect, and nothing can destroy that value. Nothing we have done can destroy that value. Nothing that anybody did to us can destroy that value because we did not do anything to get that value. You are born with value, and you never lose your basic value. Everyone in the world has value. There is nothing you can do to lose that value.

Grace gives us the freedom to heal and grow. The freedom to move beyond the mistakes of the past into a hopeful future. Feelings of shame can hinder you from doing the things that you should, the things that you could do. Grace builds up, grace encourages.

- **Shame** is a painful feeling of humiliation or distress caused by knowing a choice or behavior was wrong.

  - o **Functional shame** is a healthy response to doing something wrong or foolish. Healthy repair is to own it, confess, and ask what you can do to make it right, ask for forgiveness.
  - o **Dysfunctional shame** is the feeling that I am wrong, not that I did something wrong, but that I am a damaged human, and I am wrong.

- **Guilt** is a feeling of unease due to having done something wrong or failed in an obligation that violates a standard of conduct, especially violating law and involving a penalty.

  - o **Functional (True) guilt** is a healthy feeling that lets me know I have done wrong. Healthy repair is to confess it and ask what I can do to make it right, ask for forgiveness.
  - o **Dysfunctional (False) guilt** is the feeling that because something is wrong I must be the cause of it. Abuse victims can often feel dysfunctional guilt.

True guilt the is the guilt I feel for a wrong I have done. I feel the guilt and it can drive me to do something about the guilt.

If we confess our sins, he is faithful and just
and will forgive us our sins and
purify us from all unrighteousness.
1 John 1:9

Then I am released from the guilt. I may still have a repair to do to make it right with people, but God and I have worked it out, confession is me agreeing with God that the behavior was wrong, I repent and ask his forgiveness.

Some people feel guilty all the time. They feel guilty for anything that is wrong in the world. That false guilt can be part of the worldview that an abuser leaves with an abuse victim. The abuser tells the victim they are responsible for the way the abuser is treating them. That shifting of blame is also a part of the abuse. The victims, especially if that victim is a child, may believe that lie, because the one in power is saying it. Even after the victim has escaped the abuse, and has grown to adulthood, they still may believe that they are responsible for the abuse done to them. That is false guilt.

Freedom from guilt

Owning your own guilt is the way to be free from guilt. Examine, is the guilt truly yours? Did you have a choice in this guilty act? You are responsible for the choices you make. You are guilty of the results of that. But we do not have to stay stuck in guilt. God will cleanse us from guilt when we confess it. When somebody else says to us "you did that" trying to shame us, Grace and forgiveness means we are free from the guilt. We can say "yes, I did that. I don't do that anymore." When we try to hide from the guilt it keeps us trapped in shame, it keeps us hindered. Our growth and healing cannot fully take place where there is deceit, where there are lies, where there is a lack of forgiveness. Healing needs truth. Discretionary truth, age-appropriate truth, in the right place and time. But always truth.

Giving graceful gifts, not transactions.

There is a difference between a gift and a transaction. In a transaction, each party gets something. It is a trade. A gift, however, one person gives freely to another and there is nothing that has to be given back or traded for it.

Here is an example: You are about to enter a building, and you notice someone coming toward the door with an armload of packages. It would be difficult for them to open the door themselves, so you wait and hold the door open for them. You have given them a gift.

When they get in front of you, they do not say 'thank you' and they rush on, not even acknowledging your presence. Now you feel annoyed and mad. Well, it turns out that was not a gift after all. It was a transaction. You did not get a thank you, so you did not get paid. Therefore, you feel cheated and taken advantage of. If you had given it as a gift, it would not matter whether they said thank you or not because you gave it away freely.

Life is a lot easier when we spend it giving gifts rather than having transactions with people. When we give away freely as a gift, we feel good about that. And if they do give us a thank you, it feels even better: we got a gift back. Whether they thank us or not it is a win for us because we are doing it as a gift, not because we're going to get something back from it.

In Summary

Grace gives us the freedom to move beyond the mistakes of the past into a hopeful future. Grace builds up, grace encourages. As we have freely received grace we can freely give grace.

A grace-filled life is a pleasure.

CHAPTER 16

Building hope for a future

And we boast in the hope of the glory of God.
Not only so, but we also glory in our sufferings,
because we know that suffering produces
perseverance;
perseverance, character; and character, hope.
Romans 5:2b-4

Hope is the confident expectation of what God has promised. Hope in general is a desire for things to change for the better. It has a feeling of expectation, anticipation of positive outcomes.

Ways to build hope.

We build hope through building our character. We build character by enduring hard times. During hard times, we find that endurance is an intentional choice to do what is right in the midst of struggle. We strengthen our resolve to endure which is an exercising, strengthening of our hope.

Other ways that we build hope include listening to other people's journeys to hope. When I read through the Bible, I find it encouraging how all the heroes of the faith messed up. They did things wrong. And yet God stayed in a relationship with them, helping them to grow and to heal and to mature and to endure, helping them to have the strength and to have hope. We do not have to be perfect to have hope of God's favor.

I heard a story of a man who had gone through a tragedy, and he was going through a healing process. The way he described it was that it was like he saw the darkness trying to come and overtake him. In hope, he saw the sun and ran away from the darkness toward the light. But he could not run fast enough to stay in the sunlight because the sun was setting. The only way to make it back to the light was to turn around and walk into the darkness and endure the darkness of that grief, endure the darkness of that healing process because on the other side of the dark night comes the sunrise. The hope for the sunrise can help us walk through those dark times of healing. Going forward sometimes means turning to walk through the dark night of suffering into the sunrise of hope. We can recognize the evidence of hope if we look for it.

When we look into our own past and when we hear the stories of others who have come through hard struggles we see in those stories the hopes realized. There are many times when exactly what they hoped for was not realized and yet the overall hope of a better, more fulfilling future was realized. We will not always see the hope that is before us, but pondering those stories and the evidence of hope within them helps us to have hope.

The last time you got a new vehicle before you decided on what kind of vehicle you wanted to get, how many of that type did you notice on the roads? Probably not very many and not often, if you notice them at all. The week after you got your new vehicle, how many of that type of vehicle did you see on the roads around you? If you are like most of us, you saw lots of them. It seems like they were at every crossroads, in every parking lot. What was the difference? There were not more of them around. What happened is you became focused to look for that type of vehicle. Because you bought one. you began to notice them.

When you become focused to look for evidence of hope you will notice it everywhere. If you start writing a journal and recording the positive things, the evidence of hope, that happens every day, you will find they are all around you. Each day, write down something good about today. You will find lots of evidence and your own hope builds. There are a lot of positive things that happen every day; we just have to endure the struggle as we look for them.

Trusting God is part of that endurance. God can redeem the struggles we are experiencing. He can bring something good out of them, for ourselves, or for others. When Paul was put into prison, he had lots of time and inclination to write, and God inspired him to write lots of letters to churches and to people. We have the copies of those letters now that have taught and encouraged Christians for centuries in our Bible. We do not know how God will redeem our struggles, but I can trust that he will, even when it means trusting past what I can see at the moment.

Writing down your own story of hope is another way to strengthen your hope. What difficulties have you come through in the past? What things encouraged you during that time? How were you supported by the words or actions of others? Writing it out develops your ability to remember how you endured and that there was a time you came through your struggles.

Your personal emergency procedures manual

If you were on a journey, taking an airplane flight, flying along at 30,000 feet and one of the two engines died, the pilot has an emergency procedures manual. When is the first time you would have wanted him to look at it? Probably long before that emergency came up. You are on the journey of life. A good thing to do is to make your own emergency procedures manual for your journey, a written-out plan of how you handle the emergencies of life. I call this your personal emergency procedures manual because it shows the importance of the document.

There can be a number of parts to your personal emergency procedures manual. Let's take a look at a few of them:

- **Stories of Past Struggles Survived.** Write down ways you came through a difficult part in your past and the things that helped you.

- **Words of Affirmation.** Create a list of positive things other people have said about you.
- **Calming Images.** Write out descriptions of images that help you to feel calm. These should be positive images you can think about that will help to calm you down when things are feeling really stressful.
- **Calming Activity.** Create a list of things you can do to change your physical state and your mental-emotional state. This includes physical exercise and mental exercises. They should all be things you can do to feel better.
- **Scripture.** Copy down specific passages of scripture that stand out to you, that encourage you and bring you comfort, and hope. Physically writing them down helps them to be more alive to you.
- **Social Resources.** Make a list of people you can connect with face to face, ones you could contact when you are feeling sad or upset or when you feel like you just need to talk to somebody.
- **Exit Resources.** Where could you go if you needed to leave the situation that you were in? Where could you go if you could not sleep tonight where you slept last night?
- **What to take.** What are the important things that you would need to take with you if you had to leave suddenly? Where are these kept? Where are the originals and the copies?

There can be other parts to your personal emergency procedures manual. The reason I suggest you write it out and make it an actual physical thing is that when you are in the midst of an emergency it can be hard for you to remember all of this helpful information.

Writing all of these out helps you to feel calmer and more prepared. It reminds you that you do have resources, that you are a person of value, and you are prepared. An emergency is by its nature unexpected, so we cannot plan for it exactly, but we can make good and helpful plans. Plans may prove worthless, but the process of planning is vital. Planning helps you to go through tough times when things feel really stressful because you know there are things that you can do to help it be better.

The second item on the list is words of affirmation. I will give you your first affirmation. "I know you have courage and strength because you are reading about a healing process that is awkward and messy. That is evidence that you have already decided to explore this, or you wouldn't read this far into this book." When you write that down in the words of affirmation file, you must write it down as a quote and put a period after it. Treat that file as an evidence file. You don't get to put a comma after a quote and say something negative like "yeah but she doesn't know that I'm just reading this because I don't have anything to do today." You do not get to taint evidence. Be faithful and list the quote as spoken. Period.

Notice your level of calm or unease right now. Then pick one of the following descriptions of a calm place or make your own one like it. Think of somewhere you have been and immerse yourself for a couple of moments in the sights, sounds, smells, taste, and a touch of that calm place. Think of a natural place that you really enjoyed alone, when you went to the ocean or the beach, or up to the mountains and the trees, whatever place you enjoy. You have those positive images and with those images you are thinking about the sights and the sounds and the smells and what it feels like on your skin. A place that gives you a sense of rest from the stress. Really relax into the images. After a few minutes, again pay attention to your level of calm. What difference did you notice?

Free resource –
www.faithfulhabits.com/KeepingCalm

Audio files of these calming images being read aloud for you so you can close your eyes and just imagine the places.

Excerpt from the book

Keeping Calm: Seven key skills to being calm in the midst of troubling times.

Ocean.

The horizon spreads in a panoramic in front of you, nothing but water as far as the eye can see, till water and sky merge into a distant blur. Waves come rolling in, swells building till the wave crests and splashes over. An occasional wave grows bigger than the ones before it. They splash down and lap at your feet on the sand. The sky is a saturated blue, dotted here and there with fluffy clouds. Birds bob on the ocean. Little sandpiper birds dash in and out of the surf. Seagulls fly across the blue sky. Listen to their calls. Hear the splashing of the water around your feet. Take a deep breath, smell the salt in the air, taste the freshness of the breeze that blows through your hair, caressing your skin. Feel the water lapping at your feet and splashing. Feel the wet sand as the water rushes over you, pulling the sand out from under your feet. Turn and walk away from the water. Feel the damp sand above the waterline, how firm it is to walk on. Move on until loose, dry sand shifts with each of your steps. Notice how soft the sand and water feel and yet look at the rocks that have been polished smooth by those same elements. The entire feeling at the ocean is one of soothing peace.

Forest.

The path between the trees is narrow and dappled with sunlight and shadow. Birds flit back and forth between the trees. Their songs and the swoosh of their wings fill the air. Insects and butterflies flutter and land on leaves swaying in the breeze. Large trees are surrounded by smaller saplings and bushes. The bark of the big trees has a deeply grained texture while the bark on saplings is almost smooth. Reach out and touch it. Feel the tree against your skin. Then look up, where the undersides of the leaves sparkle as sunlight shimmers through them. Glimpse the dappled blue sky beyond the canopy. The wind blows and the leaves of different trees dance and flutter in their own unique dances. Beneath your feet lie the fallen leaves of verdant forest, rustling softly as you walk along. Here and there in the treetops, a squirrel skitters along, watching and chattering. The air smells of growing things, rich and earthy. The whole forest has a feeling of calm and peace.

Stream.

The mountain stream is crystal clear. At the bottom, rocks in beautiful colors glint in the sun. Small fish dart back and forth, playing in the flowing current. The water is cold and fresh as you splash it on your hands. It flows over rocks with a soothing and gentle babble. The long grass growing at the edge of the stream falls into the water, flowing back and forth with the current. Little water skipper bugs dance on the surface of the water. The warmth of the sun cheers your heart as you bask in this relaxing scene.

It takes time and intention to make these lovely images strong and rich enough in your memory so that you can easily access them when you are stressed. However, it's worth the effort so that you can give the memory your full attention and find relief from stress. When you take the time to be aware of and remember the details, the image becomes rich in your mind. Later, as you remember the scene, it will give you moments of rest from the day-to-day stress that you experience.

Stress tends to build and grow in intensity as the day goes on. When you take that moment of calm relief from the stress, it helps tremendously. Although the stress continues to build, that break resets the stress to a lower level, lowering the intensity of the stress and making you stronger and better able to deal with it.

Developing a "safe" spot.

For some people, a place to rest is a mental image of a safe spot. You create the image of a spot in your mind that feels calm and safe to you, a place you take pleasure in being. Whether it is a city park, neighborhood streets, an ocean or mountains or forest or stream, or a room in a home, it is a place you create for yourself to feel safe and calm. You can step away from whatever is stressing you for a moment and spend a little bit of time in that safe, calm place.

Safe Connections

When you are thinking of who to put on a list of the people you could talk to, think through both social connections and professional connections. The pastor of your church someone who leads women's ministry, a friend that you've had for a long time that you know is safe, or a therapist are all options. It helps to know you've got people you can talk to.

Think about where you could go if you needed to leave where you are and couldn't sleep there tonight. There are women's shelters and men's shelters, some that take people with their children. Do you know where those are? Do you have contact information for them? Do you have friends who might let you stay on their couch for a short period of time? Think about what kind of resources do you have.

In this section, we have looked at a number of resources you have and how you can develop them to be stronger and more available to you in a time of need. When we get very tired and stressed it can be hard to remember all the resources we have available. Taking the time to write out your own emergency procedures manual means you only have to remember one thing -where is this manual. But more than that; the very act of assembling this information and writing it out and organizing it puts the information more accessible in your brain. You will remember more of it.

Free Resource
www.faithfulhabits.com/connections.quickguide

Quick guide to developing safe connections with people.

Excerpt from Book 3 in the Trauma Healing Series

CONNECTIONS

Master the art of relationship development

In summary

Building hope is something we all can do. Hope in general is a desire for things to change for the better. It has a feeling of expectation, an anticipation of positive outcomes. We build hope through building our character. We build character by enduring hard times. We strengthen our resolve to endure which is an exercising, strengthening of our hope.

CHAPTER 17

Cleaning Out Dark Corners

There comes a time when you think you have worked through the trauma wounds of your past, but then the pain comes back. You worked hard and you thought you had resolved all the pains of the past and yet suddenly it seems like it is back the same as it was before. Was all that hard work wasted if the pain returns?

Observe the pain and distress for a few minutes. Has it come back exactly like it was before? When you take a few moments to look at it, there is a difference. Perhaps when you were working through the old wounds, the pain felt like a level 10 and hung on for two or three days at that level. You had intense emotions and memories. After you have processed through the healing, the old wound gets triggered again and the pain returns. But now it is at a level 3 and lasts for only an hour or two. You process through it again and when it gets triggered again in a year or two, it is only a level 2 and stays for only ten minutes.

It is as if you're on a spiral staircase in a tower with many windows. You look out and see the landscape below. You keep climbing and climbing and you think you have traveled a long way, but when you look out a window you see the same landscape below. You may feel discouraged that even after all that hard work it is the same view. But it is not. You are at a higher level. The landscape below is the same, but you are seeing it from a different angle.

Sometimes a new memory of trauma will surface, one you have not dealt with before from a dark corner or unexplored space. Perhaps it is coming out now because you are stronger now. You have learned the skills to work through difficult times and now you can face this one. You can put this memory to rest.

How to put a memory to rest

Painful memories of our past can be put to rest. When you have worked through memory, talked it through with your therapist, and written through it in journaling, you will see the past more objectively. You get a clearer picture of what was right and what was wrong. It becomes more evident whose fault it was and what could have been done then by whom. In putting it to rest, you will have an answer written out for each part of those memories. What is the truth you want to remind yourself about that time? Do you need to forgive? Do you need to ask for forgiveness? Do you need to confront? Do you need to protect? When you write out an event of the past and take the time to see it objectively and see what you can do now to put that memory to rest, you are changing that memory. It no longer stands alone. It now has information about what is true and what you have done to work toward healing it. When that old memory comes back, you can think about the new part that you have added to it instead of just being stuck in the pain of the old part.

Being willing to work through whatever God brings to mind when a memory comes back is a chance to take your healing to a deeper level. Think of it as your opportunity to work through the dark corners or edges of the memories of the past. You did not complete all the healing the first time through because you first had to master the big concepts. As you understand yourself and your wounds better, you work through a deeper level of healing. You are cleaning out the dirty corners, the hidden recesses. When it comes back, it is not a signal of defeat, just another opportunity to choose to forgive, to release, and to trust.

Each time you do that you are reminding yourself that you are no longer there in that trauma. That was the past and you have come a long way since then. It can be good to take the time to think about anything good that has happened in your life since that time. Focus on the good of today, the pleasures of today. The intensity of these old memories will fade.

Free resource –
www.faithfulhabits.com/KeepingCalm

How to be calmer in 10 minutes or less.

Excerpt from the book

Keeping Calm: Seven key skills to being calm in the midst of troubling times.

Not listening to lies that say you will never be free.

To be free of our past does not mean that we never remember it again. What it means is the past becomes a healed scar, not an open wound. That healed scar can be a trigger to remind us of how we have grown, that we have shown courage and resilience. Some challenges may be with us forever. Our freedom may come in a different way. Paul had his thorn in the flesh, but God's grace is sufficient to help us through those things. We can use that as a reminder to trust God, to lean on him, be free in him.

Foreground or background

In my life, I have what I call the foreground and the background of things in my mind. The things in my foreground are those items or tasks I am involved with at this moment. Then I have what is in the background of my mind. I am aware that it is there, but it does not take over my life. For instance, I have foot pain. It is just there. It is genetic and there is nothing that can be done about it. So, I just choose not to dwell on it. I'm aware that it is there, but I'm not shifting my whole life around because of it. I choose to focus on the things that are in my foreground, the pleasures that are in my life, what is fun, the relationships I treasure. I let the foot pain do whatever it is going to do, but it is in the background. We can choose to have the residual scars or discomfort of our past traumas be in the background. They do not have to shape our foreground.

In summary

Even after we think we have worked through our traumas, some memories, emotions, or thoughts may be triggered and trouble us. You are stronger now and you will be able to work through them and put them to rest easier. Live your life in the foreground, experiencing joy and hope.

CHAPTER 18

Strengthening What Remains, Choosing to Change

Create more strength

How do we create more strength in our life? When we do physical exercise, we stress the muscles, then rest them, to build strength. The muscles we exercise are the ones that grow stronger. When we have worked on healing parts of our lives and created new habits and new ways to interact in our lives, and put the old things to rest, we are choosing what we strengthen. The ones we spend time with, the ones we give a home to, the ones we feed and nurture and take care of, are the parts of our life that are going to be strengthened. It takes time to make new habits.

Depending on who you read about, some people say it takes seven days to make a new habit. Some people say it takes 30 days to create a new habit, some 60 days. I think the length of time it takes varies for each person and for each habit. Some habits are achieved quickly, and some may take months of effort. But the one constant thing is that in order to create a new habit I have to assess what habits I have and choose intentionally to do something new. I intentionally do the new habit for a while. I have to say, yes I've chosen to do this differently now. My intentional effort into the new way of responding strengthens that new habit. As we avoid the old way of responding, we weaken the old habit we are replacing.

Invariably though, one day you find you did it the old way again. Understand that doing it the old way, picking up the old habit, is not a change in direction for you. That was just a pothole in the road and so you pick yourself up out of the pothole and then get back on the road in the new direction you had decided to go. It does not mean that you have ruined your chance of doing something new.

Making of habits

Take an inventory of your strengths. This is a 5-minute exercise. Set a timer and write down a list of strengths that you have: things that that you do well, things that you can do. Some of these might be physical things, some of them might be connection things with other people, some might be skills that you know, things that you have done in your work, some are things that you understand and things you enjoy. Keep writing and use the entire five minutes.

Here is a place to STOP and do this exercise before you continue.

At the end of the five minutes, take a look at each of those strengths and write about how you developed that strength. For example, I can tie my shoes well. How did I learn to tie my shoes well? I had somebody who is knowledgeable about shoe-tying show me how, step by step. Then they coached me as I tried to do it. They corrected my missteps and coached me some more. Then I repeated those steps slowly and carefully and often with a little bit of extra coaching and help until I figured out how to do it. Then I was able to do it myself, still a little slowly. Eventually, not only am I doing it by myself, but I'm also doing it fast and well. I don't even think about it anymore. I have created and strengthened muscle memory so much that I do it automatically. I just think "tie the shoe" and I do it without any effort. If you look at how you developed the strengths that are on your list, many have likely been developed in a similar way.

Now think about two skills in your life that you want to stronger and better developed. What do you need to work on strengthening? If you need to strengthen your ability to connect with people, what can you do this week to move that forward? Maybe you take the initiative to be where people are, reach out to people, and smile and greet new people. Maybe you ask questions and are interested in their life. Ask how they're doing.

Maybe the skill you want to strengthen is your ability to read the Word of God. So, you set aside a time for that each day, even if just for five minutes. Building the habit of daily being in God's Word is more important than the length of time as you get started on a habit. The Bible is a thick book, but it's filled with smaller stories and segments. There are many reading plans suggested online and in apps. So, you look up how are you going to read this through, and you do some planning. Maybe you get some coaching about it, or find a reading buddy to help you be accountable.

Seeking new skills, more education, new interests, hobbies, or a new job is part of our growth. We were created to be creative. We seek out new experiences, learn new skills, and learn something more about the world. In the midst of doing that, you're going to be around people who are involved in the same thing that you're involved in. So, while you are learning that new skill, you also have the opportunity to build new friendships.

By allowing yourself to feel the excitement of learning new things, you get the pleasure of the feeling of competence when you become skilled. There is joy in learning new skills and when we finally have mastered it. You see this in a child when they finally master something new, like tying their shoes or learning to ride a bike.

Every skill has a point at which it feels hard. That does not mean you need to give up. Beyond that difficult spot is a sense of accomplishment, so when we have patient endurance to continue, we are reaching toward the joy of accomplishment. That is part of our restoration. We are created in God's image: to be creative.

As we explored at the beginning of this book, we are designed to heal. When you get a cut on your finger it will start a healing process right away to restore to the original design. If nothing hinders it, healing will soon take place. But if it has a sliver in it, dirt, and germs in it, your body still works toward healing, but there is matter in the way that hinders healing. The wound needs cleaning in order to have the full, healthy healing process work properly.

It is similar to mental and emotional healing. The lingering effects of past bullying, abuse, trauma, trouble, or chaos can negatively the healing process. It affects today's relationships, today's ability to make good decisions, today's ability to have joy. In order to heal properly, the trauma wounds need cleaning. Many people have experienced trauma, and problems in their life that create pain, chaos, and lingering emotional wounds. The negative patterns of behavior that follow these wounds can last for decades. The wounds are rarely healed by time alone. Understanding our original design and changing to a healthy pattern of behavior, removing the barriers that hinder, will give those wounds a good chance to heal.

Healing comes through prayer, study, connection with others, and perhaps working with a mental health counselor.

This book explores our basic design as a person of worth and the way trauma may hinder our individual healing. We are designed to have the joy of a rich emotional life and a creative mind. The hindering effects of our wounds need to be cleaned out so that we can heal as we were designed to. We looked deeply into your uniqueness and the way old wounds may have eroded your self-worth and trapped you into painful patterns of responding to life that hinder your healing. Now you have explored healthy patterns of living and how to move from wounded toward health.

Restoration was written to help you to build insight into your own inner value and to help you to learn healthy ways of functioning. As the second book in the Trauma Healing Series, Restoration gave you an in-depth look at the primary principles on which a healthy life is based, the way we are designed to function, and how to heal. The first book in the series, *Fundamentals*, gives an overview of our basic rights as a human and how trauma hinders healthy living. The other two books in the series, *Connections,* and *Abundance*, explore the foundational principles further and go deeply into the skill-building process in relationships and personal freedom in healing old wounds and moving into a pattern of healthy living.

In these pages, I shared the richness of our original design and showed how to work on removing the crippling effects of past traumas so you can heal. We looked at methods of how you can make changes to let yourself heal from the wounds of your past. You read about the fundamental principles of our original design of how we can heal and grow. If you address the emotional, physical, and intellectual principles presented in this book, you can have a healthier life. By living the principles of a healthy lifestyle, you can live your very best life, unhindered by the debilitating effects of past traumas.

My promise to you, dear reader, is that if you implement two or three of the principles found in these pages, you will find that you will experience a happier, more contented life. It will take some effort on your part, but the skills you need to develop to move forward are here in your hands. If you apply five or six of these principles, it can literally change the course of your life and have a positive effect on people around you. If you apply all the ideas in this book, you will discover a revolution inside, a return to something even more powerful than happiness. That is the presence of peace.

AFTERWORD

Faith's Story

Decades of my life were spent living with trauma. I grew up in a Christian and abusive home. Christian and abusive are two words that should not be together, but they were in my childhood experience. I grew up in the midst of extreme poverty, occasional homelessness, and all kinds of abuse. When I was beaten as a child, the physical wounds and bruises would heal after a time. But the emotional wounds on my heart stayed raw and painful.

Restoration to the original design was evident in my body's physical healing and in some parts of the emotional and mental healing. But in other parts of my mind and heart, there were lingering effects of trauma that kept those areas in a constant state of painful rawness. As I got older, I thought I had forgiven and forgotten the past, only to have some current feeling trigger the old wounds and all their uncertainty and pain.

Hard life lessons in those early years taught me the importance of kindness because I knew what it felt like to be treated unkindly. I valued gentleness because I had been treated with violence. I was wary of 'love' because it was just a word the abusers used as they were hurting me. I found joy when I was alone and in nature. Peace was around me as I enjoyed trees and flowers, wind and sky. I learned the value of patience because in that one skill I could be stronger than those who abused me. My self-control of my emotions strengthened daily as I figured out how to survive life with trauma. But outward calm is not enough. I needed the healing work of restoration.

What the original design was for head and heart was unclear to me as a child. I only knew a child's way of coping. Those resilient childhood skills worked for me when I was young, and I survived the trauma. But the childhood coping skills that helped me survive then, crippled some areas of my life as an adult. In order to heal, I needed to go back to the original design, learn what it was, and work to remove those things that were hindering my healing. Life is often a struggle, and we get wounded. But God's loving design allows us to be able to heal.

God loves me even when life is not what I like. God seems to be more concerned with my character development than with my comfort. I have a tendency to be more concerned with my comfort. I like to be comfortable, but it is during the uncomfortable times that my character can develop. In those times, I get to choose if am I going to stay true to God, true to my integrity. Am I going to do what is right and proper even when things are hard? I get to choose whether I am going to love and trust God when life is hard.

Jesus is the way. In John 3:16, it says that God so loved the world that he sent his only son that whosoever believes in him should not perish but have eternal life. I find that such a wonderfully comforting statement. The "whosoever" means that this offer is open to me and open to anybody and everybody. The offer is something we have to accept in order to have the eternal life he offers. No one is too bad or too wrong or too different. God made all of us. When we accept Jesus as Savior and Lord, we are agreeing with God that we have done wrong. So, confessing to him what we have done, then accepting him into our life as Lord and Savior, gives us salvation. The Lord part means that then I want to obey him. He is not going to make me obey him, but because I love him and he loves me, I want to obey. So, I spend time reading his Word. I spend time with his people, so I am connected and growing more like him.

This invitation to abundant life is open to anyone and everyone. Not everyone chooses to accept Jesus as Lord and Savior. But that is who he is in my life. He is my savior, my lord, my friend, and my guide to a healthy life. The principles I have been teaching you in this book will help you tremendously to find healing and have a healthier life. They will help you to understand your original design. But the deep restoration healing at your core, that comes from knowing, loving, and following Jesus.

Other books by Faith Winters

Made in the USA
Monee, IL
20 August 2021